ROBERT'S
RULES OF ORDER

Robert's Rules of Order

The Classic Manual
of
Parliamentary Procedure

PART I.
RULES OF ORDER.

A COMPENDIUM OF PARLIAMENTARY LAW, BASED UPON THE
RULES AND PRACTICE OF CONGRESS.

PART II.
ORGANIZATION AND CONDUCT
OF BUSINESS.

A SIMPLE EXPLANATION OF THE METHODS OF ORGANIZING
AND CONDUCTING THE BUSINESS OF SOCIETIES,
CONVENTIONS, AND OTHER DELIB-
ERATIVE ASSEMBLIES.

BY

GENERAL HENRY M. ROBERT,
CORPS OF ENGINEERS, U. S. A.

WITH A FOREWORD BY

JUDITH A. ROBERTS

BELL PUBLISHING COMPANY
NEW YORK

This edition was originally published in 1907.
Special material copyright © MCMLXXVIII
  by Crown Publishers, Inc.
All rights reserved.
This edition is published by Bell Publishing Company,
distributed by Crown Publishers, Inc.,
225 Park Avenue South, New York,
New York 10003

Library of Congress Cataloging in Publication Data

Robert, Henry Martyn, 1837-1923.
  Robert's Rules of order.
  Reprint of the 1907 ed. published by Scott,
Foresman, Chicago, under title: Pocket manual of rules
of order.
  CONTENTS: pt. 1. Rules of order.—pt. 2.
Organization and conduct of business.
  Includes index.
  1. Parliamentary practice.   I. Title.
II. Title: Rules of order.
JF515.R65   1978   060.4'2   78-18277
ISBN 0-517-25920-6

x w v u t

FOREWORD

The enduring principle underlying *Robert's Rules of Order* is that, though the minority shall be heard and absentees protected, the majority will decide. The *Rules* codify this principle and enable us to preserve our basic rights in both large assemblies and in small meetings. It is a fluid work, having been revised by General Henry M. Robert on numerous occasions. These changes ensure its usefulness to contemporary organizations.

In American society today, the *Rules* provide the fundamental operating procedures for meetings of all kinds, large and small. Thousands of organizations have adopted this work as their parliamentary authority. The *Rules* were based upon practices and procedures of the British Parliament and the U. S. Congress, but because of the differences between the functions and workload of the U. S. Congress and the differences among the vast majority of organizations, the *Rules* were adapted for use by all groups. As a result, *Robert's Rules of Order* is indispensable to the orderly functioning of a group's decision-making processes, because it is a rule book that has been universally accepted. It outlines all the commonly accepted procedures, including introduction of new and old business, debate and disposition of motions, creation and uses of committees, and election of officers. This book is a well organized guide for anyone who participates in meetings, committees, or structured groups.

I

The work's original intent and its present use enable an assembly to accomplish its purposes in the most efficient manner possible. To preserve the interests of a group, the rights of each individual within the group must, of necessity, be somewhat curtailed. Without limited restraints of this kind, the probability of maintaining majority rule is greatly reduced. For this reason, many of the motions, such as motions to adjourn, are undebatable. Others, like the motion to reconsider a debatable question, may not be amended. Rules of this type are practical in that they assist in avoiding long discussion of topics that are tangential to the purpose of a meeting.

Robert's Rules of Order strikes a successful balance between the preservation of individual liberties and the proper functioning of assemblies. It has been an irreplaceable tool for organizations for more than a century. Judging from the endurance of the work, we can expect it to continue to enjoy the same importance for organizations in the future.

JUDITH A. ROBERTS
May, 1978

TABLE OF CONTENTS.

		PAGE
Table of Rules Relating to Motions		8
Preface		13

Introduction.
Parliamentary Law		17
Plan of the Work		20
" Part I.		22
" Part II.		23
" Part III.		23
Definitions and Common Errors		23

Part I.—Rules of Order.

Art. I.—Introduction of Business.

§ 1. How introduced	25
2. Obtaining the floor	25
3. What precedes debate on a question	29
4. What motions to be in writing, and how they shall be divided	30
5. Modification of a motion by the mover	32

Art. II.—General Classification of Motions.

§ 6. Principal or Main motions	32
7. Subsidiary or Secondary motions	33
8. Incidental motions	34
9. Privileged motions	35

Art. III.—Motions and their Order of Precedence.

Privileged Motions.

§ 10. To fix the time to which to adjourn	36
11. Adjourn	37
12. Questions of privilege	40
13. Orders of the day	41

Incidental Motions.

14. Appeal [Questions of Order]	45
15. Objection to consideration of a question	47
16. Reading papers	48
17. Withdrawal of a motion	49
18. Suspension of the Rules	50

Subsidiary Motions.

§ 19. Lay on the table.................... 51
20. Previous Question.................. 55
21. Postpone to a certain day............ 62
22. Commit [or Refer].................. 63
23. Amend 65
24. Postpone indefinitely................ 70

Miscellaneous Motions.

25. Rescind 71
26. Renewal of a motion 71
27. Reconsideration.................... 73

Art. IV.—Committees and Informal Action.

§ 28. Committees 79
29.   "   Form of their Reports 84
30.   "   Reception   "   85
31.   "   Adoption   "   88
32. Committee of the Whole............ 93
33. Informal consideration of a question... 96

Art. V.—Debate and Decorum.

§ 34. Debate 98
35. Undebatable questions and those opening the main question to debate 101
36. Decorum in debate.................. 104
37. Closing debate, methods of.......... 106

Art. VI.—Vote.

§ 38. Voting, various modes of............ 109
39. Motions requiring more than a majority vote 116

Art. VII.—Officers and the Minutes.

§ 40. Chairman or President.............. 119
41. Clerk, or Secretary, and the Minutes... 125

Art. VIII.—Miscellaneous.

§ 42. Session............................ 131
43. Quorum 135
44. Order of Business.................. 137
45. Amendment of the Rules of Order, etc. 138

Part II.—Organization and Conduct of Business.

Art. IX.—Organization and Meetings.

§ 46. An Occasional or Mass Meeting.
   (a) Organization 139
   (b) Adoption of resolutions........... 141
   (c) Committee on   "   142
   (d) Additional Officers 146
  47. A Convention or Assembly of Delegates................................ 146
  48. A Permanent Society.
   (a) First meeting.................... 149
   (b) Second meeting.................. 152
  49. Constitutions, By-Laws, Rules of Order and Standing Rules 155

Art. X.—Officers and Committees.

§ 50. President or Chairman............... 159
  51. Secretary, or Clerk, and the Minutes... 162
  52. Treasurer.......................... 165
  53. Committees 169

Art. XI.—Introduction of Business.

§ 54. Introduction of Business............. 172

Art. XII.—Motions.

§ 55. Motions Classified according to their object............................. 174
  56. To Modify or Amend.
   (a) Amend 176
   (b) Commit or refer................ 177
  57. To Defer Action.
   (a) Postpone to a certain time....... 178
   (b) Lay on the table 178
  58. To Suppress Debate.
   (a) Previous Question............. 179
   (b) An Order limiting or closing debate 181

§ 59. To Suppress the Question.
    (a) Objection to its consideration... 182
    (b) Postpone indefinitely........... 183
    (c) Lay on the table.............. 183

60. To Consider a question the second time.
    (a) Reconsider.................... 184

61. Order and Rules.
    (a) Orders of the day 186
    (b) Special orders................. 187
    (c) Suspension of the rules........ 188
    (d) Questions of order 188
    (e) Appeal. 189

62. Miscellaneous.
    (a) Reading of papers............ 190
    (b) Withdrawal of a motion........ 190
    (c) Questions of privilege.. 190

63. To close a meeting.
    (a) Fix the time to which to adjourn....................... 191
    (b) Adjourn...................... 191

Art. XIII.—Miscellaneous.
§ 64. Debate 193
65. Forms of stating and putting questions. 194

Part III.—Miscellaneous.

§ 66. Right of an Assembly to Punish its
    members 198
67. Right of an Assembly to Eject any one
    from its place of meeting.......... 199
68. Rights of Ecclesiastical Tribunals..... 199
69. Trial of Members of Societies........ 201
70. Call of the House.................. 204
Index 209

TABLE OF RULES
RELATING TO MOTIONS.

TABLE OF RULES RELATING TO MOTIONS

[Containing Answers to Two Hundred Questions in Parliamentary Practice.]

Explanation of the Table.—A Star shows that the rule heading the column in which it stands, applies to the motion opposite to which it is placed; a blank shows that the rule does not apply; a figure shows that the rule only partially applies, the figure referring to the note showing the limitations. Take, for example, "Lay on the Table," the Table shows that §19 of the Pocket Manual treats of this motion; that it is "undebatable" and "cannot be amended;" and that an affirmative vote on it (as shown in note 5) "cannot be reconsidered;"—the four other columns containing blanks show that this motion does not "open the main question to debate," that it does not "require a ⅔ vote," that it does "require to be seconded," and that it is not "in order when another member has the floor,"

[*See page 11.*]

NOTES.

(1) Every motion in this column has the effect of suspending some rule or established right of deliberative assemblies (see note to §39), and therefore requires a two-thirds vote, unless a special rule to the contrary is adopted.

(2) Undebatable if made when another question is before the assembly.

(3) An Amendment may be either (1) by "*adding*" or (2) by "*striking out*" words or paragraphs; or (3) by "*striking out certain words and inserting others*," or (4) by "*substituting*" a different motion on the same subject; or (5) by "*dividing the question*" into two or more questions, as specified by the mover, so as to get a separate vote on any particular point or points.

(4) An Appeal is undebatable only when relating to indecorum, or to transgressions of the rules of speaking, or to the priority of business, or

Section in Pocket Manual.	Undebatable [§35].	Opens Main Question to Debate [§35].	Cannot be Amended [§23].	Cannot be Reconsidered [§27].	Requires a ⅔ Vote [§39].—See Note 1.	Does not require to be Seconded [§].	In order when another has the floor [§].
11 Adjourn	*		*	*			
10 Adjourn, Fix the Time to which to							
23 Amend [3]							
23 Amend an Amendment			*				
45 Amend the Rules					*		
14 Appeal, relating to indecorum, etc. [4]	*		*				
14 Appeal, all other cases		2	*				
14 Call to Order	*		*	*		*	*

37	Close Debate, motion to......
22	Commit or Refer......
34	Extend the Limits of Debate, motion to......
10	Fix the Time to which to Adjourn......
36	Leave to Continue Speaking after Indecorum
19	Lay on the Table......
37	Limit Debate, motion to......
15	Objection to Consideration of a Question [6]
13	Orders of the Day, motion for the......
21	Postpone to a Certain Time......
24	Postpone Indefinitely......
20	Previous Question [8]......
44	Priority of Business, questions relating to
12	Privilege, Questions of......
16	Reading Papers......
27	Reconsider a Debatable Question......
27	Reconsider an Undebatable Question......
22	Refer (same as Commit)......
25	Rescind......
11	Rise (in Committee equals Adjourn)......
33	Special Order, to make a......
18	Substitute (same as Amend)......
18	Suspend the Rules......
19	Take from the Table......
44	Take up a Question out of its Proper Order.
17	Withdrawal of a Motion......

when made while the Previous Question is pending. When debatable, only one speech from each member is permitted. On a tie vote the decision of the Chair is sustained.

(5) An affirmative vote on this motion cannot be reconsidered.

(6) The objection can only be made when the question is first introduced, before debate.

(7) Allows of but limited debate upon the propriety of the postponement.

(8) The Previous Question, if adopted, cuts off debate and brings the assembly to a vote on the pending question only, except where the pending motion is an amendment or a motion to commit, when it also applies to the question to be amended or committed.

(9) Can be moved and entered on the record when another has the floor, but cannot interrupt business then before the assembly; must be made on the day, or the day after, the original vote was taken, and by one who voted with the prevailing side.

See next page for Order of Precedence of Motions and Forms of Putting Certain Questions.

ADDITIONAL RULES TO ACCOMPANY TABLE.

Order of Precedence of Motions.

The ordinary motions rank as follows, and any of them (except to amend) can be made while one of a lower order is pending; but none can supersede one of a higher order; the Previous Question requires a two-thirds vote, the others only a majority:

Undebatable.

To Fix the Time to which to Adjourn.
To Adjourn (when unqualified).
For the Orders of the Day.
To Lay on the Table.
The Previous Question (⅔ vote).

} *Cannot be Amended.*

Debatable.

To Postpone to a Certain Time.
To Commit or Refer.
To Amend.
To Postpone Indefinitely.

} *Can be Amended.*

The motion to Reconsider can be made when any other question is before the assembly, but cannot be acted upon until the business then before the assembly is disposed of [see note 9 above], when, if called up, it takes precedence of all other motions, except to adjourn, and to fix the time to which to adjourn. Questions incidental to those before the assembly, take precedence of them and must be acted upon first.

Forms of Putting Certain Questions.

If the *Previous Question* is demanded, it is put thus: "Shall the main question be now put?" or "Shall debate be now closed, and the vote taken on the pending question?" [or "on the resolution?" or "amendment?"].

If an *Appeal* is made from the decision of the Chair, the question is put thus: "Shall the decision of the Chair stand as the judgment of the assembly [convention, society, etc.]?"

If the *Orders of the Day* are called for, the question is put thus: "Will the assembly now proceed to the Orders of the Day?"

When, upon the introduction of a question, some one *objects to its consideration*, the chairman immediately puts the question thus: "Will the assembly consider it?" or, "Shall the question be considered [or discussed]?"

If the vote has been ordered to be taken by *yeas and nays*, the question is put in a form similar to the following: "As many as are in favor of the adoption of these resolutions will, when their names are called, answer *yes* [or *aye*]—those opposed will answer *no*."

Remarks Upon the Table of Rules Relating to Motions.

The preceding Table furnishes, (1) an index to the rules relating to motions; (2) lists of the motions belonging to each of the seven classes indicated by the headings to the columns (by noticing the stars in each column); and (3) lists of the motions to which these headings in part apply, the extent to which they apply being shown in notes referred to by figures in the columns. After the Table, page 10, is a list of the most common motions, showing their order of precedence, and whether they can be amended or debated, and what vote they require—the four most important points about a motion; this list should be memorized. The peculiar form of putting certain questions is also shown. If it is desired to ascertain the proper motion to accomplish a special object, see § 55. For further information in regard to motions examine the Index under the title *Motions*.

How to Use the Table in Midst of Business.

When a motion is made, turn to the Order of Precedence of Motions, page 10, to see if it is in order. If it is in order and more information is wanted than is there furnished, look for the motion in the Table, and glance along the line to see if there are any stars in the columns. If there are no stars, then the rules at the head of the columns do not apply, and the motion is just like any resolution or amendment—that is (1) it is debatable; (2) the debate must be strictly confined to the motion; (3) it can be amended; (4) it can be reconsidered; (5) it requires a majority vote for its adoption; (6) it requires to be seconded; and (7) it is not in order when another has the floor. These general principles should be fixed in the mind and they should be strictly observed, unless a star shows that the motion is an exception to the general rule, or a figure refers to a note showing to what extent it is an exception. In this way the chairman or any other member may in a moment learn the correct rulings on all the above points.

To Illustrate—An amendment of a resolution being before the assembly, it is moved to refer it to a committee [or "to commit"]. The "Order of Precedence of Motions" shows that "to commit" is in order [because it stands above "to amend"], and the Table shows that it differs from an ordinary resolution in that it "opens to debate the main question" [that is, the original resolution]. Now if it is moved to "indefinitely postpone" the question, the chairman should rule it out of order, as he would see from a glance at the "Order of Precedence of Motions." If it is moved "to lay the question on the table," it will be found, as above, to be in order, and the table decides instantly the seven points. [See Explanation at head of Table.]

PREFACE.

A work on parliamentary law has long been needed, based, in its general principles, upon the rules and practice of Congress, but adapted, in its details, to the use of ordinary societies. Such a work should not only give the methods of organizing and conducting meetings, the duties of officers and names of ordinary motions, but should also state systematically in reference to each motion, its object and effect; whether it can be amended or debated; if debatable, the extent to which it opens the main question to debate; the circumstances under which it can be made, and what other motions can be made while it is pending. This Manual has been prepared with a hope of supplying the above information in a condensed and systematic form, each rule in Part I either being complete in itself, or giving references to every section that in any way qualifies it, so that a stranger to the work can refer to any special subject with safety.

A Table of Rules is placed immediately before this Preface, which will enable a presiding officer to decide some two hundred common and important questions of parliamentary law without turning a page.

The Second Part is a simple explanation of the common methods of conducting business in ordinary meetings. The motions are classified here according to their uses, and those used for a similar purpose are compared with each other. This part is intended for that large class in every community who are almost wholly unacquainted with parliamentary usages, and are not able to devote much study to the subject, but would be glad with little labor to learn enough to enable them to take part in meetings of deliberative assemblies without fear of being out of order.

The Third Part contains some useful information, including the legal rights of assemblies, call of the house, etc.

The object of Rules of Order is to assist an assembly to accomplish the work for which it was designed, in the best possible manner. To do this it is necessary to restrain the individual somewhat, as the right of an individual, in any community, to do what he pleases, is incompatible with the interests of the whole. Where there is no law, but every man does what is right in his own eyes, there is the least of real liberty. Experience has shown the importance of definiteness in the law; and in this country, where customs are so slightly established and the published manuals of parliamentary practice so conflicting, no society should attempt to conduct business without having adopted some work upon the subject, as the authority in all cases not covered by their own special rules.

It has been well said by one of the greatest of English writers on parliamentary law: "Whether these forms be in all cases the most rational or not is really not of so great importance. It is much more material that there should be a rule to go by, than what that rule is, that there may be a uniformity of proceeding in business, not subject to the caprice of the chairman, or captiousness of the members. It is very material that order, decency and regularity be preserved in a dignified public body."

H. M. R.

NOTE.

In the twenty-three years since the first publication of this work many questions of parliamentary law arising under these rules have been referred to the author for decision. The most important of these rulings that are not readily deducible from the text, are incorporated in the editions later than the one hundred and forty-fifth thousand, generally in the form of additional notes. [See, especially, amendments, § 23.] The necessity of renewing the electrotype plates has also been taken advantage of to make a few changes, as indicated below, which are all in the direction of more close conformity to either the usage of Congress or the fundamental principles of parliamentary law.

The changes are as follows:

(*a*) The form of putting the question on the motion to *strike out* has been changed from the old peculiar parliamentary form to the natural form used in Congress and almost universally in this country. [§ 23.]

(*b*) In *filling blanks* the *smallest* sum has been given the precedence instead of the largest, to conform to the recent revision of the U. S. Senate Rules, and the practice of the House of Representatives and Parliament. [§ 23.]

(*c*) The time for making the motion to *Reconsider* has been extended to include the next day, provided a meeting is held thereon, to conform to the practice of the House of Representatives.

(*d*) The allowing the making at the same time

of the motions to *reconsider* and *lay the motion to reconsider on the table,* has been stricken out as an unnecessary violation of the principle that only one motion can be made at a time.

(*e*) To *extend the limits of debate* has been included in the motions requiring a two-thirds vote, because it is a suspension of a rule or an order of the assembly.

INTRODUCTION.

Parliamentary Law.

Parliamentary Law refers originally to the customs and rules of conducting business in the English Parliament; and thence to the customs and rules of our own legislative assemblies. In England these usages of Parliament form a part of the unwritten law of the land, and in our own legislative bodies they are of authority in all cases where they do not conflict with existing rules or precedents.

But as a people we have not the respect which the English have for customs and precedents, and are always ready for such innovations as we think are improvements, and hence changes have been and are constantly being made in the *written* rules which our legislative bodies have found best to adopt. As each house adopts its own rules, it results that the two houses of the same legislature do not always agree in their practice; even in Congress the order of precedence of motions is not the same in both houses, and the Previous Question is admitted in the House of Representatives, but not in the Senate. As a consequence of this, the exact method of conducting business in any particular legislative body is to be obtained only from the Legislative Manual of that body.

The vast number of societies, political, literary,

scientific, benevolent and religious, formed all over the land, though not legislative, are deliberative in character, and must have some system of conducting business, and some rules to govern their proceedings, and are necessarily subject to the common parliamentary law where it does not conflict with their own special rules. But as their knowledge of parliamentary law has been obtained from the usages in this country, rather than from the customs of Parliament, it has resulted that these societies have followed the customs of our own legislative bodies, and our people have thus been educated under a system of parliamentary law which is peculiar to this country, and yet so well established as to supersede the English parliamentary law as the common law of ordinary deliberative assemblies.

The practice of the National House of Representatives should have the same force in this country as the usages of the House of Commons have in Engand, in determining the general principles of the common parliamentary law of the land; but it does not follow that in every matter of detail the rules of Congress can be appealed to as the common law governing every deliberative assembly. In these matters of detail, the rules of each House of Congress are adapted to their own peculiar wants, and are of no force whatever in other assemblies. But upon all great parliamentary questions, such as what motions can be made, what is their order of precedence, which can be debated, what is their effect, etc., the common law of the land is settled by the practice of the United States House of Representatives, and not by that of the English Parliament, the United States Senate, or any other body.

While in extreme cases there is no difficulty in deciding the question as to whether the practice of Congress determines the common parliamentary law, yet between these extremes there must necessarily be a large number of doubtful cases upon which there would be great difference of opinion, and to avoid the serious difficulties always arising from a lack of definiteness in the law, every deliberative assembly should imitate our legislative bodies in adopting Rules of Order for the conduct of their business.*

---

* Where the practice of Congress differs from that of Parliament upon a material point, the common law of this country follows the practice of Congress. Thus in every American deliberative assembly having no rules for conducting business, the motion to adjourn would be decided to be undebatable, as in Congress, the English parliamentary law to the contrary notwithstanding: so if the Previous Question were negatived, the debate upon the subject would continue as in Congress, whereas in Parliament the subject would be immediately dismissed; so too, the Previous Question could be moved when there was before the assembly a motion either to amend, to commit, or to postpone definitely or indefinitely, just as in Congress, notwithstanding that, according to English parliamentary law, the Previous Question could not be moved under such circumstances.

When the rules of the two Houses of Congress conflict, the House of Representatives rules are of greater authority than those of the Senate in determining the parliamentary law of the country, just as the practice of the House of Commons, and not the House of Lords, determines the parliamentary law of England. For instance, though the Senate rules do not allow the motion for the Previous Question, and make the motion to postpone indefinitely take precedence of every other subsidiary motion [§ 7] except to lay on the table, yet the parliamentary law of the land follows the practice of the House of Represen-

Plan of the Work.

This Manual is prepared to partially meet this
want in deliberative assemblies that are not legislative in their character. It has been made sufficiently complete to answer for the rules of an
assembly until they see fit to adopt special rules
conflicting with and superseding any of its rules
of detail, such as the Order of Business [§ 44],
etc. Even in matters of detail the practice of
Congress is followed, wherever it is not manifestly unsuited to ordinary assemblies; and in

---

tatives in recognizing the Previous Question as a
legitimate motion, and assigning to the very lowest
rank the motion to postpone indefinitely.

But in matters of detail, the rules of the House
of Representatives are adapted to the peculiar wants
of that body, and are of no authority in any other
assembly. No one, for instance, would accept the
following House of Representatives rules as common
parliamentary law in this country: 'That the chairman, in case of disorderly conduct, would have the
power to order the galleries to be cleared; that the
ballot could not be used in electing the officers of an
assembly: that any fifteen members would be author-
ized to compel the attendance of absent members and
make them pay the expenses of the messengers sent
after them; that all committees not appointed by the
chair would have to be appointed by ballot, and if
the required number were not elected by a majority
vote, then a second ballot must be taken in which a
plurality of votes would prevail; that each member
would be limited in debate upon any question to one
hour; that a day's notice must be given of the introduction of a bill, and that before its passage it must
be read three times, and that without the special
order of the assembly it cannot be read twice the
same day. These examples are sufficient to show the
absurdity of the idea that the rules of Congress in all
things determine the common parliamentary law.

such cases, in Part I, there will be found, in a footnote, the Congressional practice. In the important matters referred to above, in which the practice of the House of Representatives settles the common parliamentary law of the country, this Manual strictly conforms to such practice.*

The Manual is divided into three distinct parts, each complete in itself, and a Table of Rules [see

* On account of the party lines being so strictly drawn in Congress, no such thing as harmony of action is possible, and it has been found best to give a bare majority in the House of Representatives (but not in the Senate) the power to take final action upon a question without allowing of any discussion. In ordinary societies more regard should be paid to the rights of the minority, and a two-thirds vote be required, as in this Manual, for sustaining an objection to the introduction of a question, or for adopting a motion for the Previous Question, or for adopting an order closing or limiting debate. [See note to § 39 for a discussion of this question.] In this respect the policy of the Pocket Manual is a mean between those of the House and Senate. But some societies will doubtless find it advantageous to follow the practice of the House of Representatives, and others will prefer that of the Senate. It requires a majority, according to this Manual, to order the ayes and nays [§ 38], which is doubtless best in most assemblies; but in all bodies in which the members are responsible to their constituents, a much smaller number should have this power. In Congress it requires but a one-fifth vote, and in some bodies a single member can require a vote to be taken by yeas and nays.

Any society adopting this Manual should make its rules govern them in all cases to which they are applicable, and in which they are not inconsistent with the By-Laws and Rules of Order of the society. [See § 49 for the form of a rule covering this case.] Their own rules should include all of the cases where it is desirable to vary from the rules in the Manual, and especially should provide for a Quorum [§ 43] and an Order of Business [§ 44], as suggested in these rules.

page 8] containing a large amount of information in a tabular form, for easy reference in the midst of the business of a meeting.

Part I contains a set of Rules of Order systematically arranged, as shown in the Table of Contents. Each one of the forty-five sections is complete in itself, so that one unfamiliar with the work cannot be misled in examining any particular subject. Cross references are freely used to save repeating from other sections, and by this means the reader, without using the index, is referred to everything in the Rules of Order that has any bearing upon the subject he is investigating. The references are by sections, and for convenience the numbers of the sections are placed at the top of each page. The motions are arranged under the usual classes, in their order of rank, but in the Index under the word *motion* will be found an alphabetical list of all the motions generally used.

The following is stated in reference to each motion:

(1) Of what motions *it takes precedence* (that is, what motions may be pending, and yet it be in order to make and consider this motion).

(2) To what motions it *yields* (that is, what motions may be made and considered while this motion is pending).

(3) Whether it is *debatable* or not (all motions being debatable unless the contrary is stated).

(4) Whether it can be *amended* or not.

(5) In case the motion can have no subsidiary motion *applied* to it, the fact is stated [see Adjourn, § 11, for an example: the meaning is, that

the particular motion, to adjourn, for example, cannot be laid on the table, postponed, committed or amended].

(6) The *effect* of the motion if adopted, whenever it could possibly be misunderstood.

(7) The *form of stating the question* when peculiar, and all other information necessary to enable one to understand the question.

Part II is a Parliamentary Primer, giving very simple illustrations of the methods of organizing and conducting different kinds of meetings, stating the very words used by the chairman and speakers in making and putting various motions; it also gives, briefly, the duties of the officers, and forms of minutes and of reports of the treasurer and committees; it classifies the motions into eight classes according to their object, and then takes up separately each class and compares those in it, showing under what circumstances each motion should be used.

Part III consists of a few pages devoted to miscellaneous matters that should be understood by members of deliberative assemblies, such as the important but commonly misunderstood subjects of the Legal Rights of Deliberative Assemblies and Ecclesiastical Tribunals, etc.

Definitions and Common Errors.

In addition to the terms defined above (*taking precedence of, yielding to* and *applying to,* see p. 22), there are other terms that are liable to be misunderstood, to which attention should be called.

Meeting and *Session.* For the distinction between these terms, see first note to § 42.

Previous Question. The effect of this much misunderstood motion is briefly stated in the eighth note to the Table of Rules, p. 8; a full explanation is given in § 20.

Substitute. This motion is one form of an amendment. The five forms of an amendment are shown in the third note to the Table of Rules, p. 8, and are more fully explained in § 23.

Shall the Question be Discussed? is a common form in some societies of stating the question on the consideration of a subject. It is very apt to convey a wrong impression of its effect, which is, if negatived, to dismiss the question for that session, as shown in § 15.

Accepting a Report, which is the same as adopting it, is confounded by many with receiving a report. [See note to § 30 for common errors in acting upon reports.]

The terms *Congress* and *H. R.*, when used in this Manual, refer to the U. S. House of Representatives.

The word *Assembly,* when occurring in forms of motions (as in an Appeal, § 14), should be replaced by the special term used to designate the particular assembly—as, for instance, "Society," or "Convention," or "Board."

PART I.

—

RULES OF ORDER.*

—

Art. I. Introduction of Business.
[§§ 1-5.]

1. All business should be brought before the assembly by a motion of a member, or by the presentation of a communication to the assembly. It is not usual, however, to make a motion to receive the reports of committees [§ 30] or communications to the assembly; and in many other cases in the ordinary routine of business, the formality of a motion is dispensed with; but should any member object, a regular motion becomes necessary.

2. Before a member can make a mo-

---

* If the reader's knowledge of the elementary details of parliamentary practice is not sufficient for him to understand these rules in Part I, he should, before proceeding further, read Part II, which is essentially a Parliamentary Primer. [See the first note to § 46.]

tion or address the assembly upon any question, it is necessary that he *obtain the floor;* that is, he must rise and address the presiding officer by his title, thus: "Mr. Chairman," who will then announce the member's name.* Where two or more rise at the same time, the chairman must decide who is entitled to the floor, which he does by announcing that member's name. In making his decision he should be guided by the following principles:

(*a*) The member upon whose motion the subject under discussion was brought before the assembly (or, in case of a committee's report, the one who presented the report), is entitled to be recognized as having the floor (if he has not already had it during that discussion) notwithstanding another member may have first risen and addressed the chair.

(*b*) No member who has once had the floor is again entitled to it while the same question is before the assembly, provided the floor is claimed by one who has not spoken

---

* If the chairman has some other title, as President, Moderator, etc., he is addressed by his special title, thus: "Mr. President." [See § 34.] If the chairman rises to speak before the floor has been assigned to any one, it is the duty of a member who may have previously risen to take his seat. [See Decorum in Debate, § 36.]

to that question.* (c) As the interests of
the assembly are best subserved by allowing
the floor to alternate between the friends
and enemies of a measure, the chairman,
when he knows which side of a question is
taken by each claimant of the floor, and
their claim is not determined by the above
principles, should give the preference to the
one opposed to the last speaker.

From this decision of the chairman any
two members can make an appeal [§ 14].†
Where there is doubt as to who is entitled
to the floor, the chairman can at the first
allow the assembly to decide the question by
a vote—the one getting the largest vote
being entitled to the floor.

After the floor has been assigned to a
member he cannot be interrupted by calls for
the question,‡ or by a motion to adjourn, or
for any purpose, by either the chairman or

---

* See § 26 for an explanation of what is necessary
to technically change the question before the assembly.

† In the U. S. House of Representatives there is
no appeal from the decision of the chair as to who
is entitled to the floor, nor should there be any appeal
in such cases in large assemblies, especially in mass
meetings, as the best interests of the assembly require
the chair to be given more power in such large
bodies.

‡ It is a plain breach of order when a member has
the floor for any one to call for the question or an
adjournment; and the chairman should protect the
speaker in his right to address the assembly.

any member, except (*a*) to have entered on the minutes a motion to reconsider [§ 27] ; (*b*) by a question of order [§ 14] ; (*c*) by an objection to the consideration of the question [§ 15] ; (*d*) by a call for the orders of the day [§ 13],* or (*e*) by a question of privilege that requires immediate action, as shown in § 12.

In such cases the member, when he rises and addresses the chair, should state at once for what purpose he rises, as, for instance, that he "rises to a point of order."

NOTE ON OBTAINING THE FLOOR.—The chair should not recognize a member who has risen and remained standing while another member is speaking, provided anyone else rises after the speaker has yielded the floor.

When a member obtains the floor and makes a debatable motion that is in order, if it is not immediately seconded, the chair should inquire if the motion is seconded (which can be done by any member, without rising or addressing the chair, simply saying, "I second it"), and the maker of the motion should then be regarded as having the refusal of the floor in preference to all other members. No motion made after his should be recognized until the chair has given ample time for members to respond to the invitation for a second, and if the motion is seconded, until after the maker of the motion has had an opportunity to claim the floor. Motions to adjourn and to lay on the table are frequently made

---

* See close of first note to § 13.

by persons who have not the floor, and after another motion has been made, and while the maker of the latter motion is entitled to the floor. The chair should not recognize such motions.

A member submitting a report of a committee, or offering a resolution, does not lose the floor by requesting the Secretary to read the report or resolution, and the Secretary has not obtained the floor thereby, nor can the chair entertain a motion made by him, unless the member expressly yields the floor for the motion. As soon as the reading is finished the member who submits the report resumes the floor and moves its adoption, when the chair, after stating the question, recognizes the gentleman as having the floor. Of course motions that are in order when another has the floor could interrupt the member at any time.

3. Before any subject is open to debate [§ 34] it is necessary, first, that a motion be made by a member who has the floor; second, that it be seconded (see exceptions below) ; and third, that it be stated by the presiding officer.* When the motion is in writing it shall be handed to the chairman, and read before it is debated.

This does not prevent suggestions of alterations, before the question is stated by the presiding officer. To the contrary, much

---

* Examples of the various forms of making motions are given in §§ 46, 54. Forms of stating questions will be found in § 65. Any member can second any motion from his seat without rising or addressing the chair. In Congress, motions are not required to be seconded.

time may be saved by such informal remarks; which, however, must never be
allowed to run into debate. The member
who offers the motion, until it has been
stated by the presiding officer, can modify
his motion, or even withdraw it entirely;
after it is stated he can do neither, without
the consent of the assembly [see §§ 5, 17].
When the mover modifies his motion, the
one who seconded it can withdraw his second.

Exceptions: A call for the orders of the
day, a question of order (though not an appeal), or an objection to the consideration
of the question [§§ 13, 14, 15], does not
have to be seconded; and many questions of
routine are not seconded or even made; the
presiding officer merely announcing that, if
no objection is made, such will be considered the action of the assembly.

4. All Principal Motions [§ 6], Amendments and Instructions to Committees,
should be in writing, if required by the presiding officer. Although a question is com-
plicated, and capable of being made into several questions, no one member (unless there
is a special rule allowing it) can insist upon
its being divided; his resource is to move
that the question be divided, specifying in

his motion how it is to be divided. Anyone else can move as an amendment to this, to divide it differently.

This *Division of a Question* is really an amendment [§ 23], and subject to the same rules. Instead of moving a division of the question, the same result can be usually attained by moving some other form of an amendment. When the question is divided, each separate question must be a proper one for the assembly to act upon, even if none of the others were adopted. Thus, a motion to "commit with instructions" is indivisible ; because, if divided, and the motion to commit should fail, then the other motion to instruct the committee would be improper, as there would be no committee to instruct.*   The

---

* The 46th Rule of the House of Representatives requires the division of a question on the demand of one member, provided "it comprehends propositions in substance so distinct that one being taken away, a substantive proposition shall remain for the decision of the House."   But this does not allow a division so as to have a vote on separate items or names.   The 121st Rule expressly provides that on the demand of one-fifth of the members a separate vote shall be taken on such items separately, and others collectively, as shall be specified in the call, in the case of a bill making appropriations for internal improvements.   But this right to divide a question into items extends to no case but the one specified.   The common parliamentary law allows of no division except when the assembly orders it, and in ordinary assemblies this rule will be found to give less trouble than the Congressional one.

motion to "strike out certain words and insert others" is indivisible, as it is strictly one proposition.

5.   After a question has been stated by the presiding officer, it is in the possession of the assembly for debate; the mover cannot withdraw or modify it, if anyone objects, except by obtaining leave from the assembly [§ 17], or by moving an amendment.*

Art. II.   General Classification of Motions.†

[§§ 6-9.]

6.   A Principal or Main Question or

---

* Rule 40 H. R. is as follows: "After a motion is stated by the Speaker, or read by the Clerk, it shall be deemed to be in the possession of the House, but it may be withdrawn at any time before a decision or amendment." The practice under this rule has been, not to allow a motion to be withdrawn after the previous question has been seconded. This manual conforms to the old parliamentary principle, which is probably better adapted to ordinary societies. In certain organizations it will, doubtless, be found advisable to adopt a special rule like the Congressional one just given.

† In § 54, the ordinary motions will be found classified according to their object.

Motion* is a motion made to bring before the assembly, for its consideration, any particular subject. No Principal Motion can be made when any other question is before the assembly. It takes precedence of nothing, and yields to all Privileged, Incidental and Subsidiary Questions [§§ 7, 8, 9].

7. **Subsidiary or Secondary Motions** are such as are applied to other motions, for the purpose of most appropriately disposing of them.† They take precedence of a Principal Question, and must be decided before the Principal Question can be acted upon. They yield to Privileged and Incidental Questions, [§§ 8, 9,] and are as follows (being arranged in their order of precedence among themselves):

---

* No motion is in order that conflicts with the Constitution, By-Laws, or Standing Orders or Resolutions of the assembly, or any resolution already adopted during the session [§ 42], and if adopted it is null and void. In order to introduce such a motion it is necessary to amend the Constitution or By-Laws, or to rescind the rule or resolution [§ 25]. To reconsider is not a principal motion.

† Take, for example, a motion that an appeal lay on the table: to lay on the table is a subsidiary motion enabling the assembly to properly dispose of the appeal; while the appeal is an incidental question, arising out of a decision of the chair, to which some members objected.

Lay on the Table.................. See § 19
The Previous Question............ "   § 20
Postpone to a Certain Day........ "   § 21
Commit, or Refer, or Re-Commit.... "   § 22
Amend .... "   § 23
Postpone Indefinitely .... "   § 24

Any of these motions (except to Amend) can be made when one of a lower order is pending, but none can supersede one of a higher order. They cannot be applied* to one another except in the following cases : (*a*) the Previous Question applies to the motions to Postpone, without affecting the principal motion, and can, if specified, be applied to a pending amendment [§ 20]; (*b*) the motions to Postpone to a certain day, to Commit and to Amend, can be amended; and (*c*) a motion to Amend the minutes can be laid on the table without carrying the minutes with it [§ 19].

8. Incidental Questions are such as arise out of other questions, and, consequently take precedence of, and are to be decided before, the questions which give rise to them. They yield to Privileged Questions [§ 9] and cannot be amended. Excepting

---

* See page 22 for explanation of some of these technical terms.

an Appeal they are undebatable; an Appeal is debatable or not, according to circumstances, as shown in § 14. They are as follows:

Appeal (or Questions of Order)... See § 14
Objection to the Consideration of a
  Question .... " § 15
The Reading of Papers............ " § 16
Leave to Withdraw a Motion...... " § 17
Suspension of the Rules.......... " § 18

9. Privileged Questions are such as, on account of their importance, take precedence of all other questions whatever, and on account of this very privilege they are undebatable [§ 35], excepting when relating to the rights of the assembly or its members, as otherwise they could be made use of so as to seriously interrupt business. They are as follows (being arranged in their order of precedence among themselves):

To Fix the time to which the As-
  sembly shall Adjourn ....,..... See § 10
Adjourn .... " § 11
Questions relating to the Rights and
  Privileges of the Assembly or any
  of its Members .... " § 12
Call for the Orders of the Day..... " § 13

Art. III.   Motions and their Order of Precedence.*

[§§ 10-27.]

Privileged Motions.

[§§ 10-13; see § 9.]

10. **To fix the time to which the Assembly shall Adjourn.** This motion takes precedence of all others, and is in order even after the assembly has voted to adjourn, provided the chairman has not announced the result of the vote. If made when another question is before the assembly, it is undebatable [§ 35]; it can be amended by altering the time. If made when no other question is before the assembly, it stands as any other principal motion, and is debatable.† The *Form* of this motion is, "When this assembly adjourns, it adjourns to meet at such a time."

---

* For a list of all the ordinary motions, arranged in their order of precedence, see the Table of Rules. page 10. All the Privileged and Subsidiary ones in this article are so arranged.

† In ordinary societies it is better to follow the common parliamentary law, and permit this question to be introduced as a principal question, when it can be debated and suppressed [§§ 58, 59] like other questions. In Congress it is never debatable, and has entirely superseded the unprivileged and inferior motion to "adjourn to a particular time."

11. To Adjourn. This motion (when unqualified) takes precedence of all others, except to "fix the time to which to adjourn," to which it yields. It is not debatable, it cannot be amended or have any other subsidiary motion [§ 7] applied to it; nor can a vote on it be reconsidered. If qualified in any way, it loses its privileged character, and stands as any other principal motion. The motion to adjourn can be repeated if there has been any intervening business, though it be simply progress in debate [§ 26].* When a committee is through with any business referred to it, and prepared to report, instead of adjourning, a motion should be made "to rise," which motion, in committee, has the same privileges as to adjourn in the assembly [§ 32].

The *Effect upon Unfinished Business* of an adjournment is as follows† [see Session, § 42] :

---

* See Note at close of this Section.

† "After six days from the commencement of a second or subsequent session of any Congress, all bills, resolutions and reports which originated in the House, and at the close of the next preceding session remained undetermined, shall be resumed, and acted on in the same manner as if an adjournment had not taken place."—Rule 136 H. R. But unfinished business does not go over from one Congress to another Congress. Any ordinary society that meets as seldom as once a year, is apt to be composed of as different membership at its successive meetings as any two

(*a*) When it does not close the session, the business interrupted by the adjournment is the first in order after the reading of the minutes at the next meeting, and is treated the same as if there had been no adjournment;* an adjourned meeting being legally the continuation of the meeting of which it is an adjournment.

(*b*) When it closes a session in an assembly which has more than one regular session each year, then the unfinished business shall be taken up at the next succeeding session previous to new business, and treated the same as if there had been no adjournment [see § 44 for its place in the order of business]. Provided that, in a body elected for a definite time (as a board of directors elected for one year), unfinished business shall fall to the ground with the expiration of the term for which the board or any portion of them were elected.

(*c*) When the adjournment closes a session in an assembly which does not meet

---

successive Congresses, and only trouble would result from allowing unfinished business to hold over to the next yearly meeting.

* Of course the assembly may adopt rules that modify this general rule, as in the case of the motion to Reconsider [§ 27] in these rules.

more frequently than once a year, or when the assembly is an elective body, and this session ends the term of a portion of the members, the adjournment shall put an end to all business unfinished at the close of the session. The business can be introduced at the next session, the same as if it had never been before the assembly.

NOTE ON ADJOURNMENT.—The motion to adjourn cannot be made when another has the floor, nor after a question has been put and the assembly is engaged in voting, but it is in order after the vote has been taken and before it has been announced. In this latter case when the business is resumed, the vote should be announced. In some societies a great deal of time is consumed in counting the ballots at the annual elections, and in such cases it would often be advantageous to take a short recess, or else transact other business until the tellers are ready to report. A motion could be made, "That when we adjourn, we adjourn to meet at the call of the chair," and then when this is adopted the society could adjourn, the chair calling the society to order as soon as the ballots are counted. Or, the object could be accomplished by voting to take a *Recess* of, say, fifteen minutes, which is equivalent to the above two motions, and would be in order at any time except when either of them is pending. A Recess is an adjournment of the assembly for a limited time during its session.

The assembly may vote down the motion to adjourn in order to hear one speech or take one vote, and, therefore, it must have the privilege of being renewed when there has been any prog-

ress in the business or the debate. But the chair
should not allow this high privilege to be abused
to the annoyance of the assembly, and, therefore,
should refuse to entertain the motion to adjourn
when the assembly has just voted it down, and
nothing has occurred since to show the assembly
has any wish to adjourn.

No Appeal or Questions of Order should be
entertained after the motion to adjourn has been
made, unless the assembly refuses to adjourn,
when they would be in order.

12. Questions of Privilege.* Questions
relating to the rights and privileges of the
assembly, or any of its members, take precedence of all other questions, except the two
preceding, to which they yield. If the question is one requiring immediate action it can
interrupt a member's speech. When such a
question is raised the chairman decides
whether it is a question of privilege or not,
from which decision an appeal [§ 14] can
be taken by any two members.

It is not necessary that the assembly take
final action upon the question of privilege
when it is raised—it may be referred to a
committee [§ 22], or laid on the table [§

---

* Questions of Privilege must not be confounded
with Privileged Questions; the latter include the
former, and several other questions as shown in § 9.
Disorder in the gallery, one member opening a window
so as to cause a draft, endangering the health of
others, charges made against the official character
of a member, etc., are examples of questions of privilege.

19], or it may have any other subsidiary
[§ 7] motion applied to it, and in such case
the subsidiary motion is exhausted on it
without affecting the question interrupted
by the question of privilege. As soon as the
latter is disposed of, the assembly resumes
the consideration of the question which it
interrupted.

13. Orders of the Day. A call for the
Orders of the Day takes precedence of every
other motion, excepting to Reconsider [§
27], and the three preceding, to which latter
three it yields, and is not debatable, nor can
it be amended. It does not require to be seconded, and it is in order when another member has the floor.*

When one or more subjects have been

---

* Rule 54 H. R. provides that at the close of the
morning hour (which is devoted to reports from committees and resolutions) a motion is in order to proceed to "the business on the Speaker's table, and to
the orders of the day;" it then specifies the order in
which the business on the Speaker's table shall be
considered, and closes thus: "The messages, communications and bills on his table having been disposed of,
the Speaker shall then proceed to call the orders of
the day." While in Congress it is not in order to
interrupt a member to call for the orders of the day,
yet it is the practice to permit a member, at the close
of the morning hour, even though another member has
the floor, to move to proceed to "the business on the
Speaker's table, and to the orders of the day." To
apply the above principle to ordinary assemblies, it is
necessary to allow a motion for the orders of the day
to interrupt a member who may have the floor, after
the time has arrived for their consideration.

assigned to a particular day or hour, they
become the Orders of the Day for that day
or hour, and they cannot be considered before that time, except by a two-thirds vote
[§ 39]. And when that day or hour arrives,
if called up, they take precedence of all but
the three preceding questions [§§ 10, 11,
12] and a reconsideration [§ 27]. Instead
of considering them, the assembly may appoint another time for their consideration.
If not taken up on the day specified, the
order falls to the ground.

The orders of the day are divided into two
classes, Special Orders and General Orders,
the first class always taking precedence of
the latter. *General Orders* can be made by
a majority, by postponing questions to certain times, or by adopting a programme or
order of business for the day or session;
these General Orders cannot interfere with
the established rules of the assembly. A
Special Order suspends all the rules of the
assembly that interfere with its consideration
tion at the times specified,* and it therefore

---

* Thus, if an assembly had a rule like that in §
44 for the order of business, when the time appointed
for the Special Order arrived, any one could call for
the Special Orders, even though a Committee were
reporting at the time; but the orders for the day in
general could not be called for until all the Committees' reports had been acted upon.

requires a two-thirds vote to make any question a Special Order. [This motion is in order whenever a motion to Suspend the Rules [§ 18] is in order. After one Special Order is made for a certain time, it is not in order to make another Special Order to precede or interfere with it, but a Special Order can interfere with General Orders.

When the Orders of the Day are taken up, it is necessary to take up first the Special Orders, if there are any, and then the General Orders; in each class the separate questions must be taken up in their exact order, the one first assigned to the day or hour taking precedence of one afterwards assigned to the same day or hour. (A motion to take up a particular part of the Orders of the Day, or a certain question, is not a privileged motion.) Any of the subjects, when taken up, instead of being then considered, can be assigned to some other time, a majority being competent to postpone even a Special Order.

The *Form* of this question, as put by the chair when the proper time arrives, or on the call of a member, is, "Shall the Orders of the Day be taken up?" or, "Will the assembly now proceed to the Orders of the Day?"

The *Effect* of an *affirmative vote,* on a call for the Orders of the Day, is to remove the question under consideration from before the assembly, the same as if it had been interrupted by an adjournment [§ 11].

The *Effect* of a *negative vote* is to dispense with the orders merely so far as they interfere with the consideration of the question then before the assembly.

A common case of Orders of the Day is where an assembly has adopted an order of business for the day, specifying the hour at which each question shall be considered. When the hour appointed for taking up the second question has arrived, the chairman should announce that fact, and, if no one objects, immediately put to vote the questions before the assembly, and state the question next to be considered. Should any member object to this, the chairman should at once submit to the assembly a question like this: "Will the assembly now proceed to consider [here state the subject], which was assigned to this hour?" While a programme, as here supposed, does not state the fact, yet its very form implies that at the expiration of the time allowed any subject, all the questions then pending shall be put to vote. Still, as it takes a formal vote, except by unanimous consent, to proceed originally to the Orders of the Day, so a formal vote is necessary if anyone objects to take up the next order, and close discussion on the one pending.

Incidental Motions.

[§§ 14-18; see § 8.]

14. Appeal [Questions of Order].* A Question of Order takes precedence of the question giving rise to it, and must be decided by the presiding officer without debate. If a member objects to the decision, he says, "I appeal from the decision of the chair." If the appeal is seconded, the chairman immediately states the question as follows: "Shall the decision of the chair stand as the judgment of the assembly?"† If there is a tie vote the decision of the chair is sustained.

This appeal yields to Privileged Questions

---

* A motion cannot be ruled out of order after it has been entertained and debated without objection. An appeal can be made only at the time of the decision of the chair.

† The word Assembly can be replaced by Society, Convention, Board, etc., according to the name of the organization. See § 65 for a fuller explanation of the method of stating the question on an Appeal.

[§ 9]. It cannot be amended; it cannot be debated when it relates simply to indecorum [§ 36], or to transgressions of the rules of speaking, or to the priority of business, or if it is made while the previous question [§ 20] is pending. When debatable, no member is allowed to speak but once, and whether debatable or not, the presiding officer, without leaving the chair, can state the reasons upon which he bases his decision. The motion to Lay on the Table* [§ 19], and the Previous Question [§ 20] if the appeal is debatable, can be applied to an appeal, and when adopted they affect nothing but the appeal. The vote on an appeal may also be reconsidered [§ 27]. An appeal is not in order when another appeal is pending.

It is the duty of the presiding officer to enforce the rules and orders of the assembly, without debate or delay. It is also the right of every member, who notices a breach of a rule, to insist upon its enforcement. In such case he shall rise from his seat, and say, "Mr Chairman, I rise to a point of order." The speaker should immediately take his

---

* In Congress, the usual course in case of an Appeal is to lay it on the table, as this practically kills it and sustains the chair.

seat, and the chairman requests the member to state his point of order, which he does, and resumes his seat. The chair decides the point, and then, if no appeal is taken, permits the first member to resume his speech. If the member's remarks are decided to be improper, and anyone objects to his continuing his speech, he cannot continue it without a vote of the assembly to that effect.

Instead of the method just described, it is usual, when it is simply a case of improper language used in debate, for a member to say, "I call the gentleman to order;" the chairman decides whether the speaker is in or out of order, and proceeds as before. The chairman can ask the advice of members when he has to decide questions of order, but the advice must be given sitting, to avoid the appearance of debate: or the chair, when unable to decide the question, may at once submit it to the assembly.

15. Objection to the Consideration of a Question. An objection can be made to the consideration of any principal motion [§ 6], but only when it is first introduced, before it has been debated. It is similar to a question of order [§ 14], in that it can be made while another member has the floor, and does not require a second; and as the chairman can call a member to order, so can he put this question, if he deems it necessary, upon his own responsibility. It cannot be debated [§ 35], or amended [§ 23], or have any other subsidiary motion [§ 7] applied to it. When a motion is made and any member "objects to its consideration," the chairman shall immediately put the question, "Will the assembly consider it?" or, "Shall the question be considered [or discussed]?" If decided in the negative by a two-thirds vote [§ 39], the whole matter is dismissed for that session [§ 42]; otherwise the discussion continues as if this question had never been made.

The *Object* of this motion is not to cut off debate (for which other motions are provided, see § 37), but to enable the assembly to avoid altogether any question which it may deem irrelevant, unprofitable or contentious.*

16. **Reading Papers.** [For the order of precedence, see § 8.] Where papers are

---

* In Congress, the introduction of such questions could be temporarily prevented by a majority vote under the 41st Rule of the House of Representatives, which is as follows: "Where any motion or proposition is made, the question, 'Will the House now con-

laid before the assembly, every member has a right to have them once read before he can be compelled to vote on them, and whenever a member asks for the reading of any such paper evidently for information, and not for delay, the chair should direct it to be read, if no one objects. But a member has not the right to have anything read (excepting as stated above) without getting permission from the assembly. The question upon granting such permission cannot be debated or amended.

17. Withdrawal of a Motion. [For order of precedence, see § 8.] When a question is before the assembly and the mover wishes to withdraw or modify it, or substitute a different one in its place, if no one objects, the presiding officer grants the per-

sider it?' shall not be put unless it is demanded by some member, or is deemed necessary by the Speaker." [See note at close of § 39.]   The English use the "Previous Question" for a similar purpose [see note at close of § 20].

The question of consideration is seldom raised in Congress, but in assemblies with very short sessions, where but few questions can or should be considered, it seems a necessity that two-thirds of the assembly should be able to instantly throw out a question they do not wish to consider. A very common form, in ordinary societies, of putting this question, is, "Shall the question be discussed?"   The form to which preference is given in the rule conforms more to the Congressional one, and is less liable to be misunderstood.

mission; if any objection is made, it will be
necessary to obtain leave to withdraw,* etc.,
on a motion for that purpose. This motion
cannot be debated or amended. When a
motion is withdrawn, the effect is the same
as if it had never been made.

18. Suspension of the Rules.† [For
the order of precedence, see § 8.] This motion is not debatable, and cannot be amended, nor can any subsidiary [§ 7] motion be
applied to it, nor a vote on it be reconsidered
[§ 27], nor a motion to suspend the rule for
the same purpose be renewed [§ 26] at the
same meeting, though it may be renewed
after an adjournment, though the next meeting be held the same day.‡ The rules of the
assembly shall not be suspended except for a
definite purpose, and by a two-thirds vote;
nor shall any rule be suspended, unless by

---

* In Congress, a motion may be withdrawn by the
mover, before a decision or amendment [Rule 40 H.
R.]. Nothing would be gained in ordinary societies
by varying from the old common law as stated above
[see note to § 5].

† This motion applies only to Rules of Order or
Standing Rules [§ 49, note], as the Constitution and
By-Laws cannot be suspended even by unanimous consent, unless they provide for their own suspension,
which should never be done except in case of a particular by-law relating to the transaction of business,
and then it should be specified.

‡ In Congress it cannot be renewed the same day.

unanimous consent, that gives any right to
a minority as small as one-third.*

The *Form* of this motion is, "to suspend
the rules which interfere with," etc., specifying the object of the suspension.

Subsidiary Motions.

[§§ 19-24; see § 7.]

19. To Lay on the Table.† This motion takes precedence of all other Subsidiary
Questions [§ 7], and yields to any Privileged [§ 9] or Incidental [§ 8] Question.
It is not debatable, and cannot be amended
or have any other subsidiary motion [§ 7]
applied to it, nor can an affirmative vote on
it be reconsidered [§ 27]. It removes the
subject from consideration till the assembly
vote to take it from the table.

The *Form*‡ of this motion is, "I move to
lay the question on the table," or, "that it be
laid on the table," or, "that the question lie

---

* There would be no use in a rule allowing one-
fifth of the members present to order the yeas and
nays, for instance, if two-thirds of those present
could suspend the rule [see the last notes to §§ 38,
39].

† See Note at close of this Section.

‡ A motion to lay a question on the table for a
specified time should not be ruled out of order but
should be recognized and stated by the chair as a
motion to postpone to a definite time. The motion to
lay on the table cannot be limited in any way.

on the table." When it is desired to take the
question up again, a motion is made, either
*to take the question from the table,** or "to
now consider such and such a question;"
which motion has no privilege and is undebatable, and cannot have any subsidiary
motion applied to it.

The *Object* of this motion is to postpone
the subject in such a way that it can be
taken up at any time, either at the same or
some future meeting, which could not be accomplished by a motion to postpone, either
definitely or indefinitely. It is also frequently used to suppress a question [§ 59] for the
session, which it does, provided a majority
vote can never be obtained to take it from
the table during that session [§ 42].

The *Effect* of this motion† is in general to
place on the table for that entire session
[§ 42] everything that adheres to the subject; so that if an amendment be ordered to
lie on the table, the subject which it is pro-

---

* In organizations whose sessions do not last longer
than a day, and are as frequent as monthly, it should
be allowed to take from the table any question laid
on the table at the previous session [§ 42]. With a
resolution it would generally be better to offer it
anew.

† A question of privilege [§ 12] does not adhere to
the subject it may happen to interrupt, and consequently if laid on the table does not carry with it the
question pending when it was raised.

posed to amend goes there with it. The following cases are exceptional: (*a*) An appeal [§ 14] being laid on the table, has the effect of sustaining, at least for the time, the decision of the chair, and does not carry the original subject to the table. (*b*) So when a motion to reconsider [§ 27] a question is laid on the table, the original question is left just where it was before the reconsideration was moved. (*c*) An amendment to the minutes being laid on the table does not carry the minutes with it.

Even after the ordering of the Previous Question up to the moment of taking the last vote under it, it is in order to lay upon the table the questions still before the assembly.

NOTE ON LAYING ON THE TABLE.—This motion has high privileges, outranking every debatable question, and being undebatable itself and requiring only a majority vote for its adoption, because it is for the best interests of the assembly that it have the power to instantly lay aside any business to attend to something more urgent. The fundamental principles of parliamentary law require that every motion which suppresses a question for the session should be open to free debate [note at close of § 35], unless debate is limited or closed by at least a two-thirds vote [note at close of § 39]. In assemblies having short sessions lasting for only a few hours, a bare majority can lay on the table every objectionable ques-

tion and thus suppress it without permitting debate. This is an abuse of the motion that often
interferes with the harmony of voluntary organizations. The reasons for giving it such high
privileges are based on the theory that the question is to be laid aside only temporarily. The motion is very valuable if used for its legitimate
purpose, but if used habitually to suppress questions, then it should require a two-thirds vote.

The minority has no remedy for the unfair
use of this motion, but the evil could be slightly
diminished as follows: The person who intro-
duces a resolution is sometimes cut off from
speaking by the motion to lay the question on
the table being made as soon as the chair states
the question, or even before. In such cases the
introducer of the resolution should always claim
the floor, to which he is entitled [note at close
of § 2], and make his speech. Persons are commonly in such a hurry to make this motion that
they neglect to address the chair and obtain the
floor. In such case one of the minority should
address the chair quickly, and, if not given the
floor, make the point of order that he is the first
one to address the chair and that the other member not having the floor was not entitled to make
a motion.

As motions laid on the table are merely temporarily laid aside, the majority should remem-
ber that the minority may all stay to the moment
of final adjournment and then be in the majority
and take up and pass the resolutions laid on the
table. The safer and fairer method is to object
to the consideration of the question [§ 15] if it is
so objectionable that it is not desired to allow
even its introducer to speak on it; or if there has
been debate so it cannot be objected to, then
move the Previous Question, which, if adopted,

immediately brings the assembly to a vote. These are legitimate motions for getting at the sense of the members at once as to whether they wish the subject discussed, and as they require a two-thirds vote for their adoption, no one has a right to object to their being made.

This motion, to lay on the table, cannot be applied to more than the question then before the meeting and whatever necessarily adheres to it. Thus, it is improper to lay on the table "Reports of Committees," or "Unfinished Business," when they are reached in the order of business. The object sought by such motions can only be attained by "suspending the rules" [18], which requires a two-thirds vote, or by laying on the table each successive report as it comes up for action.

20. The Previous Question* takes precedence of every debatable question [§ 35], and yields to Privileged [§ 9] and Incidental [§ 8] Questions, and to the motion to Lay on the Table [§ 19]; and after the demand for the previous question up to the time of taking final action under it, it is in

---

* The Previous Question is a technical name for this motion, conveying a wrong impression of its import, as it has nothing to do with the subject previously under consideration. To demand the previous question is equivalent in effect to moving "That debate now cease, and the assembly immediately proceed to vote on the pending question" [or "questions" in some cases, as shown above under the *effect* of the previous question]. So when the chairman puts the question, "Shall the main question be now put?" it means "Shall the pending question be now put?" [or "questions," as just stated]. The origin of this question, and the changes that have taken place in its effects, are described in the note at the close of this section. See § 37 for the motion to *Limit Debate*.

order to move an adjournment or that the main question be laid on the table. It is not debatable, and cannot be amended or have any other subsidiary [§ 7] motion applied to it. It applies to questions of privilege [§ 12] as well as to any other debatable questions. It is allowable for a member to submit a resolution and at the same time move the previous question thereon. It may be reconsidered,* but not after it is partly executed. It shall require a two-thirds† vote for its adoption.

When a member calls for the previous question, and the call is seconded, the presiding officer must immediately put the question, "Shall the main question be now put?" If it fails, the discussion continues as if this motion had not been made.

If adopted, its *Effect* is as follows: [See

---

* Usually but a single vote is taken in reconsidering the previous question, thus: "Will the assembly reconsider the motion ordering the previous question?" If decided affirmatively the question is divested of the previous question. This is reasonable, as the previous question is undebatable and cuts off debate, and therefore no one would vote to reconsider it who is not in favor of re-opening the debate.

† In the House of Representatives it must be seconded by a majority [to avoid the yeas and nays], and then it can be adopted by a majority vote; in the U. S. Senate it is not allowed. It is sometimes called the "gag law," which name is deserved when a bare majority can adopt it. The right of debate should be considered as an established rule of every deliberative assembly, which cannot be interfered with excepting by a vote that is competent to suspend any other rule. [See note to § 39.]

the illustration near the close of this section].

(1) Its effect [excepting when to Amend or to Commit is pending] is to instantly close debate,* and bring the assembly to a vote upon the pending question. This vote being taken, the effect of the previous question is exhausted, and the business before the assembly stands exactly as if the vote on the pending motion had been taken in the usual way, without having been forced to it by the previous question; so if this vote is reconsidered [§ 27] the question is divested of the previous question, and is again open to debate.

(2) Its effect when either of the motions to Amend [§ 23] or to Commit [§ 22] is pending, is to cut off debate, and to force a vote, not only upon the motions to amend and to commit, but also upon the question to be amended or committed.† The chair-

* After debate is closed upon a question which has been reported from a committee, the member reporting the measure has the right to make the closing speech. [See § 34.]

† If we consider the motion to amend and to commit as inseparably connected with the question to be amended or committed, so that together they constitute but one question, then it would be correct to say that the only effect of adopting the Previous Question is to cut off debate and to force the assembly to vote upon the *one question pending*. This will to many be the easiest way to look at this question, and it makes it as simple as adopting an order closing debate [§ 37 (d)], as the latter would have the same privileges, and therefore the same complications as the Previous Question.

man puts to vote all these questions in their order of precedence, beginning with the one last moved [see illustrations further on]. The previous question is not exhausted until votes have been taken on all these questions, or else it has been voted to refer the subject to a committee. If one of these votes is reconsidered before the previous question is exhausted, the pendency of the previous question precludes debate upon the motion reconsidered.

The motion for the previous question may be limited to the pending amendment, and if adopted, debate is closed on the amendment only. After the amendment is voted on, the main question is again open to debate and amendment. [In this case the form of the question would be similar to this, "Shall the question be now put on the amendment?"*] So in the same manner it can be moved on an amendment of an amendment.

The *Object* of the previous question is to bring the assembly to a vote on the question before it without further debate.†

An Appeal [§ 14] from the decision of

---

* Or thus: "Shall the debate now close and the question [or vote] be taken on the amendment?"

† For other methods of closing debate see §§ 37. 38.

the chair is undebatable [§ 35] if made after the previous question has been moved, and before final action has been taken under it.

To *Illustrate the Effect* of the previous question under all kinds of circumstances, take the following examples:

(*a*) Suppose a question is before the assembly, and an amendment to it offered, and then it is moved to postpone [§ 21] the question to another time: the previous question now being ordered stops the debate and forces a vote on the pending question—the postponement. When that vote is taken the effect of the previous question is exhausted. If the assembly refuses to postpone the subject, the debate is resumed upon the pending amendment.

(*b*) Suppose the subject under consideration is interrupted by a question of privilege [§ 12], and it has been moved to refer this latter question to a committee: the previous question being now ordered brings the assembly to a vote first on the motion to commit, and if that motion fails, next on the privileged question. After the privileged question is voted on, the previous question is exhausted, and the consideration of the subject which was interrupted is resumed.

(*c*) Suppose, again that while an amendment to the question is pending a motion is
made to refer the subject to a committee,
and some one moves to amend this last
motion by giving the committee instructions; in addition to the main question we
have here only the motions to amend and to
commit, and therefore the previous question,
if ordered, applies to them all as one question. The chairman immediately puts the
question (1) on the committee's instructions, (2) on the motion to commit, and if
this is adopted the subject is referred to the
committee and the effect of the previous
question is exhausted; but if it fails, next
(3) on the amendment, and finally (4) on
the main question.

NOTE ON THE PREVIOUS QUESTION.—Much of
the confusion heretofore existing in regard to
the Previous Question has arisen from the great
changes which this motion has undergone. As
originally designed, and at present used in the
English Parliament, the previous question was
not intended to suppress debate, but to suppress
the main question, and therefore, in England,
it is always moved by the enemies of the measure, who then vote in the negative. It was first
used in 1604, and was intended to be applied only
to delicate questions; it was put in this form,
"Shall the main question be put?" and being
negatived, the main question was dismissed for
that session. Its form was afterwards changed to

this, which is used at present, "Shall the main question be *now* put?" and if negatived the question was dismissed, at first only until after the ensuing debate was over, but now, for that day. The motion for the previous question could be debated; when once put to vote, whether decided affirmatively or negatively, it prevented any discussion of the main question, for, if decided affirmatively, the main question was immediately put, and if decided negatively (that is, that the main question be not now put), it was dismissed for the day.

Our Congress has gradually changed the English Previous Question into an entirely different motion, so that, while in England, the mover of the previous question votes against it, in this country he votes for it. At first the previous question was debatable, and if it was negatived the main question was dismissed for the day, as in England. Congress, in 1805, made it undebatable, and in 1860 caused the consideration of the subject to be resumed if the previous question was negatived, thus completely changing it from the English motion. At first its effect was to cut off all motions except the main question, upon which a vote was immediately taken. This was changed in 1840 so as to bring the House to a vote first upon pending amendments, and then upon the main question. In 1848 its effect was changed again so as to bring the House to a vote upon the motion to commit if it had been made, then upon amendments reported by a committee, if any, then upon pending amendments, and finally upon the main question. In 1860 Congress decided that the only effect of the previous question, if the motion to postpone were pending, should be to bring the House to a direct vote on the postponement—thus preventing the previous question from cutting off any pending motion, and completing the change this motion had been gradually undergoing. The previous question is now a simple motion to close debate and proceed to voting as described in the above section.

[To prevent the introduction of any improper or useless subject in an ordinary assembly in this country, the proper course is to "object to its consideration" [§ 15] when it is first introduced, which is very similar to the English previous question.]

21. To Postpone to a Certain Day. This motion takes precedence of a motion to Commit, or Amend, or Indefinitely Postpone, and yields to any Privileged [§ 9] or Incidental [§ 8] Question, and to the motion to Lie on the Table, or for the Previous Question. It can be amended by altering the time, and the Previous Question can be applied to it without affecting any other motions pending. It allows of very limited debate [§ 35], and that must not go into the merits of the subject matter any further than is necessary to enable the assembly to judge of the propriety of the postponement.

The *Effect* of this motion is to postpone the entire subject to the time specified until which time it cannot be taken up except by a two-thirds vote [§ 13]. When that time arrives it is entitled to be taken up in preference to everything except Privileged

Questions. Where several questions are postponed to different times and are not reached then, they shall be considered in the order of the times to which they were postponed. It is not in order to postpone to a time beyond that session [§ 42] of the assembly, except* to the day of the next session, when it comes up with the unfinished business, and consequently takes precedence of new business [§ 44]. If it is desired to hold an adjourned meeting to consider a special subject, the time to which the assembly shall adjourn [§ 10] should be first fixed before making the motion to postpone the subject to that day.

22. To Commit or Refer [or Recommit, as it is called when the subject has been previously committed]. This motion takes precedence of the motions to Amend or Indefinitely Postpone, and yields to any Privileged [§ 9] or Incidental [§ 8] Question, and also to the motion to Lie on the Table, or for the Previous Question, or to Postpone to a certain day. It can be amended by altering the committee, or giving it instructions. It is debatable, and opens to de-

---

* In Congress a motion cannot be postponed to the next session, but it is customary in ordinary societies.

bate [§ 35] the merits of the question it is
proposed to commit.

The *Form* of this motion is, "to refer the
subject to a committee." When different
committees are proposed they should be
voted on in the following order: (1) committee of the whole [§ 32], (2) a standing
committee, and (3) a special (or select)
committee. The number of a committee is
usually decided without the formality of a
motion, as in filling blanks [§ 23] : the chairman asks "Of how many shall the committee consist?" and a question is then put upon
each number suggested, beginning with the
smallest. The number and kind of the committee need not be decided till after it has
been voted to refer the subject to a committee.

If the committee is a select one, and the
motion does not include the method of appointing it, and there is no standing rule on
the subject, the chairman inquires how the
committee shall be appointed, and this is
usually decided informally. Sometimes the
chair "appoints," in which case he names
the members of the committee and no vote
is taken upon them; or the committee is
"nominated" either by the chair or members
of the assembly (no member nominating

more than one except by general consent), and then they are all voted upon together, except where more nominations are made than the number of the committee, when they shall be voted upon singly.

Where a committee is one for action (a committee of arrangements for holding a public meeting, for example), it should generally be small, and no one placed upon it who is not favorable to the proposed action; and if any such should be appointed, he should ask to be excused. But when the committee is for deliberation or investigation, it is of the utmost importance that all parties be represented on it, so that in committee the fullest discussion may take place, and thus diminish the chances of unpleasant debates in the assembly.

In ordinary assemblies, by judicious appointment of committees, debates upon delicate and troublesome questions can be mostly confined to the committees, which will contain the representative members of all parties. [See Committees, § 28.]

23. To Amend. This motion takes precedence of nothing but the question which it is proposed to amend, and yields to any Privileged [§ 9], Incidental [§ 8], or Subsidiary [§ 7] Question, except to Indefinitely Postpone. It can be applied to all motions except those in the list at the end of this section, which cannot be amended. It can be amended itself, but this "amendment of an amendment" cannot be amended.

An amendment may be inconsistent with one already adopted, or may directly conflict with the spirit of the original motion, but it must have a direct bearing upon the subject of that motion. *To illustrate:* a motion for a vote of thanks could be amended by striking out "thanks" and inserting "censure;" or one condemning certain customs could be amended by adding other customs.

An amendment may be in any of the following forms: (*a*) to *"add"* or *"insert"* certain words or paragraphs; (*b*) to *"strike out"* *certain words or paragraphs, and if this fails it does not preclude any other amendment than the identical one that has been rejected; (*c*) to *"strike out certain words and insert others,"* which motion is indivisible,† and if lost does not preclude

---

* It was formerly customary to state the question on a motion to strike out, thus: "Shall these words stand as a part of the resolution?" In this country it is now treated the same as any other motion.

† In the case of a motion to "strike out A and insert B," while it is indivisible, in amending it, it is considered as two questions, the amendment to the first part, the part to be stricken out, having the precedence. [U. S. Senate Rule 18.]

another motion to strike out the same words
and insert different ones; (*d*) to *"substitute"* another resolution or paragraph on the
same subject for the one pending; (*e*) to
"divide the question" into two or more
questions as the mover specifies, so as to get
a separate vote on any particular point or
points [see § 4].

If a paragraph is inserted it should be
perfected by its friends previous to voting
on it, as when once inserted it cannot be
struck out or amended except by adding to
it.   The same is true in regard to words to
be inserted in a resolution, as when once inserted they cannot be struck out, except by
a motion to strike out the paragraph, or
such a portion of it as shall make the question an entirely different one from that of
inserting the particular words.   The principle involved is, that when the assembly
has voted that certain words shall form a
part of a resolution, it is not in order to
make another motion which involves exactly the same question as the one it has decided.   The only way to bring it up again is
to move a Reconsideration [§ 27] of the
vote by which the words were inserted.

Filling Blanks* are usually treated somewhat differently from other amendments, in
that any number of members may propose,
without a second, different numbers for filling the blank, and these are treated not as
amendments of one another, but as independent propositions to be voted on suc-
cessively, the smallest sum and longest time
being put first.

Nominations are treated in a similar manner, so that a second nomination is not regarded as an amendment of the first, but as
an independent motion to be voted on if the
first fails to receive a majority vote. Any
number of nominations can be made, the
chairman announcing each name as he hears
it, and they should be voted for in the order
announced until one receives a vote sufficient for election, which is a majority unless the By-Laws prescribe a different number.

The numbers prefixed to paragraphs are
only marginal indications, and should be
corrected, if necessary, by the clerk, without any motion to amend.

---

* In the U. S. House of Representatives filling blanks
are treated as other amendments. The practice of
the Senate, as that of the English Parliament, is given
above. The Senate, until the last revison of its rules,
gives precedence to the largest instead of the smallest
sum.

An Amendment to Rules of Order, By-Laws or a Constitution shall require previous notice and a two-thirds vote for his adoption [see § 45].

[For amending reports of Committees and propositions containing several paragraphs, see § 31; for amending minutes, see § 41; for the proper form of stating the question on an amendment, see § 65.]

The following motions *cannot be amended*:

To Adjourn (when unqualified) . . . . See	"	§ 11
For the Orders of the Day	"	§ 13
All Incidental Questions	"	§ 8
To Lay on the Table	"	§ 19
For the Previous Question	"	§ 20
An Amendment of an Amendment . .	"	§ 23
To Postpone Indefinitely	"	§ 24
To Reconsider	"	§ 27

NOTE ON AMENDMENTS.—A resolution is amended by altering the words of the resolution; an amendment is amended by altering the words of the amendment, that is, by altering the words to be inserted or to be stricken out. The form of the motion cannot be amended; that is, a motion to adopt a resolution cannot be amended so as to substitute a motion to reject the resolution, as this alters the form, not the words of the resolution; a motion to "strike out A" cannot be amended by adding "and insert B," so as to read, "strike out A and insert B," which is another form of amendment, and is not an alteration of "A"; a motion to "insert B before the word C" in a resolution, cannot be amended by substituting another resolution for the one amendment pending, thus changing the form of the amendment and not simply altering "B"; a motion to "insert B before the word C" cannot be amended by adding "and D before the word E," because the only thing that can be altered in the pending amendment is "B," the other words being those that are necessary to describe what it is proposed to do with "B."

If the pending amendment is to "insert A B C D before F," it is in order to apply any form of amendment to "A B C D," and no amendment is in order that is not confined to simply altering those words, "A B C D."

When a member desires to move an amendment that is not in order at the time but affects the pending question, he should state his intention of offering his amendment if the pending amendment is voted down. In this way those who favor his amendment will vote in the negative, and if they succeed in killing it, then the new amendment can be offered.

24. To Postpone Indefinitely. This motion takes precedence of nothing except the Principal Question [§ 6], and yields to any Privileged [§ 9], Incidental [§ 8], or Subsidiary [§ 7] Motion, except to Amend. It can be applied to nothing but a Principal Question [§ 6] and a Question of Privilege [§ 12]. It cannot be amended; it opens to debate the entire question which it is proposed to postpone. Its effect* is to entirely

---

* An affirmative vote on this question is identical in effect with a negative vote on the main question. Its only value is when the opposition is doubtful of its

remove the question from before the assembly for that session [§ 42]. The Previous Question [§ 20], if ordered when this motion is pending, applies only to it without affecting the main question.

Miscellaneous Motions.

[§§ 25-27.]

25. Rescind. When an assembly wishes to annul some action it has previously taken and it is too late to reconsider [§ 27] the vote, the proper course to pursue is to Rescind the objectionable resolution, order, or other proceeding. This motion has no privilege but stands on a footing with a new resolution. Any action of the body can be rescinded regardless of the time that has elapsed.*

26. Renewal of a Motion. When any Principal Question [§ 6] or Amendment has been once acted upon by the assembly, it

strength, because if defeated on this motion they still have an opportunity for further struggle for victory, which would not be the case if they had been defeated on a vote on the main question.

* Where it is desired not only to rescind the action but to express very strong disapproval, legislative bodies have on rare occasions voted to rescind the objectionable resolution and expunge it from the record, which is done by crossing out the words, or drawing a line around them, and writing across them the words "Expunged by order of the assembly, etc.," giving the date of the order.

cannot be taken up again at the same session [§ 42] except by a motion to Reconsider [§ 27], and when the motion to reconsider has been once acted upon, it, the motion to reconsider, cannot be repeated on the same question unless the question was amended when previously reconsidered. A correction of the minutes [§ 41], however, can be made without a motion to reconsider, at the same or any subsequent session, and so can a motion to rescind [§ 25]. The motion to Adjourn [§ 11] can be renewed if there has been progress in debate, or any business transacted. As a general rule the introduction of any motion that alters the state of affairs makes it admissible to renew any Privileged or Incidental Motion (excepting a motion for the Orders of the Day or for the Suspension of the Rules as provided in §§ 13, 18), or Subsidiary Motion (excepting an Amendment), as in such a case the real question before the assembly is a different one.

To illustrate: a motion that a question lie on the table having failed, suppose afterwards it be moved to refer the matter to a committee, it is now in order to move again that the subject lie on the table; but such a motion would not be in order if it were not made till after the failure of the motion to commit, as the question then resumes its previous condition. So, if a subject has been taken from the table or an objection to its consideration has been voted down, it is not in order to move to lay it on the table, as this practically involves the very question the assembly has just decided.

When a subject has been referred to a committee which reports at the same meeting, the matter stands before the assembly as if it had been introduced for the first time. A motion which has been withdrawn has not been acted upon, and therefore can be renewed.

27. **Reconsider.** It is in order at any time, even when another member has the floor, or while the assembly is voting on the motion to Adjourn, during the day on which a motion has been acted upon, or the next succeeding day,* to move to "Reconsider the vote" and have such motion "entered on the record," but it cannot be considered while another question is before the

---

* If the vote is not reconsidered on the day it was taken, and no meeting is held the next day, then it cannot be reconsidered at the next meeting. The proper course then is to renew the motion if it failed, or rescind [§ 25] it if it had been adopted.

assembly. It must be made, excepting when the vote is by ballot, by a member who voted with the prevailing side;* for instance, in case a motion fails to pass for lack of a two-thirds vote, a reconsideration must be moved by one who voted against the motion.

A motion to reconsider the vote on a Subsidiary [§ 7] Motion takes precedence of the main question. It yields to Privileged [§ 9] Questions (except for the Orders of the Day) and Incidental [§ 8] Questions.

This motion can be *applied*† to the vote on every other question, except to Adjourn and to Suspend the Rules, and an affirmative vote on to Lay on the Table or to Take from the Table [§ 19], and a vote electing to office one who is present and does not decline. No question can be twice reconsidered,‡ unless it was amended after its first

---

* Any one can second the motion. In Congress any one can move a reconsideration, excepting where the vote is taken by yeas and nays [§ 38], when the rule above applies.

† It is not the practice to reconsider an affirmative vote on the motion to lay on the table, as the same results can be reached by the motion to take from the table. For a similar reason, an affirmative vote on a motion to take from the table cannot be reconsidered.

‡ The minutes can be corrected any number of times without a reconsideration.

reconsideration. If an amendment to a motion has been either adopted or rejected, and then a vote taken on the motion as amended, it is not in order to reconsider the vote on the amendment until after the vote on the original motion has been reconsidered. If the Previous Question [§ 20] has been partly executed, it cannot be reconsidered. If anything which the assembly cannot reverse has been done as the result of a vote, then that vote cannot be reconsidered. This motion cannot be amended; it is debatable or not, just as the question to be reconsidered is debatable or undebatable [§ 35]; when debatable, it opens up for discussion the entire subject to be reconsidered, and the Previous Question [§ 20], if ordered while it is pending, affects only the motion to reconsider. It can be laid on the table [§ 19], in which case, the reconsideration, like any other question, can be taken from the table, but possesses no privilege.* The mo-

---

* In Congress it is usual for the member in charge of an important bill as soon as it passes to move its reconsideration, and at the same time to move that the motion to reconsider be laid on the table. If the latter motion is adopted it is deemed a finality, as the number of bills on the calendar precludes its ever being taken up except by a two-thirds vote. But this is not so in an ordinary society. There is no good

tion to reconsider being laid on the table does not carry with it the pending measure.

The *Effect of making* this motion is to suspend all action that the original motion would have required until the reconsideration is acted upon; but if it is not called up, its effect terminates with the session [§ 42], provided,* that in an assembly having regular meetings as often as monthly, if there is not held upon another day an adjourned meeting of the one at which the reconsideration was moved, its effect shall not terminate till the close of the next succeeding session [see note at end of this section] But the reconsideration of an Incidental [§ 8] or Subsidiary [§ 7] Motion (except where the vote to be reconsidered had the effect to remove the whole subject from before the assembly) shall be immediately acted upon, as otherwise it would prevent action on the main question.†

While this motion is so highly privileged as far as relates to having it entered on the

reason in this case for violating the general principle that only one motion can be made at a time.

*In Congress the effect always terminates with the session, and it cannot be called up by any one but the mover, until the expiration of the time during which it is in order to move a reconsideration.

† Thus, suppose the motion to Indefinitely Postpone is negatived, showing that the assembly wish to consider the subject; if it is moved to reconsider the last

minutes, yet the reconsideration of another question cannot be made to interfere with the discussion of a question before the assembly, but as soon as that subject is disposed of, the reconsideration, if called up,* takes precedence of everything except the motions to adjourn, and to fix the time to which to adjourn. As long as its effect lasts (as shown above), any one can call up the motion to reconsider, and have it acted upon —excepting that when its effect extends beyond the meeting at which the motion was made, no one but the mover can call it up at that meeting.

The *Effect of the adoption* of this motion is to place before the assembly the original question in the exact position it occupied before it was voted upon; consequently no one can debate the question reconsidered

---

vote, then the reconsideration must be immediately acted upon, as otherwise the whole subject would be removed from before the assembly as shown above, without any possible benefit to the assembly. If the object is to prevent a temporary majority from adopting a resolution, the proper course is to wait until the resolution is finally acted upon, and then move the reconsideration. If the motion to Indefinitely Postpone is carried, the subject is removed from before the assembly, and consequently there is no hinderance to business in permitting the reconsideration to hold over to another day.

* When the reconsideration has been called up it can be treated as other motions, and holds over as unfinished business.

who had previously exhausted his right to debate [§ 34] on that question; his only resource is to discuss the question while the motion to reconsider is before the assembly. When a vote taken under the operation of the previous question is reconsidered, the question is then divested of the previous question, and is open to debate and amendment, provided the previous question had been exhausted [see § 20] by votes taken on all the questions covered by it, before the motion to reconsider was made.

A reconsideration requires only a majority vote, regardless of the vote necessary to adopt the motion reconsidered. [For reconsidering in committee see § 28.]

Note on Reconsider.—In the English Parliament a vote once taken cannot be reconsidered, but in our Congress it is allowed to move a reconsideration of the vote on the same or succeeding day, and after the close of the last day for making the motion, anyone can call up the motion to reconsider, so that this motion cannot delay action more than two days, and the effect of the motion, if not acted upon, terminates with the session. There seems to be no reason or good precedent for permitting merely two persons, by moving a reconsideration, to suspend for any length of time all action under resolutions adopted by the assembly, and yet where the delay is very short the advantages of reconsideration overbalance the evil.

Where a permanent society has meetings weekly or monthly, and usually only a small proportion of the society is present, it seems best to allow a reconsideration to hold over to another meeting, so that the society may have notice of what action is about to be taken. To prevent the motion being used to defeat a measure that cannot be deferred till the next regular meeting, it is provided that in case the society adjourns, to meet on a different day, then the reconsideration will not hold over beyond that session; this allows sufficient delay to notify the society, while, if the question is one requiring immediate action, the delay cannot extend beyond the day to which it adjourns. The rule provides that the adjourned meeting must be held on another day, in order to prevent the whole object of the reconsideration being defeated by an immediate adjournment to meet again in a few minutes. Where the meetings are only quarterly or annual the society should be properly represented at each meeting, and their best interests are subserved by following the practice of Congress, and letting the effect of the reconsideration terminate with the session.

Art. IV. Committees and Informal Action.

[§§ 28-33.]

28. Committees.* It is usual in deliberative assemblies, to have all preliminary work in the preparation of matter for their

---

* An ex-officio member of a committee or Board is one who is a member by virtue of holding some particular office. If the office is under the control of the Society, then there is no distinction between the ex-

action done by means of committees. These
may be either "standing committees"
(which are appointed for the session [§ 42],
or for some definite time, as one year) ; or
"select committees," appointed for a special
purpose; or a "committee of the whole" [§
32], consisting of the entire assembly. [For
method of appointing committees of the
whole, see § 32; other committees, see Commit, § 22.] The first person named on a
committee is chairman (in his absence the
next named member becomes chairman, and
so on), and should act as such, unless the
committee, by a majority of its number,
elects another chairman, which it is competent to do, unless the assembly has appointed the chairman. The clerk should
furnish him, or some other member of the
committee, with notice of the appointment
of the committee, giving the names of the

---

officio member and the other members. But if the
ex-officio member is not under the authority of the
Society, he has all the privileges but none of the obli-
gations of membership; as where the Governor of a
State is ex-officio a manager or a trustee of a private
academy. Sometimes the By-laws provide that the
President shall be ex-officio a member of every committee; in such a case it is evidently the intention to
permit, not to require, him to act as a member of the
various committees, and therefore in counting a quorum he should not be counted as a member. The
President is not a member of any committee except
by virtue of a special rule, unless he is so appointed
by the assembly.

members, the matter referred to them, and
such instructions as the assembly have decided upon. The chairman shall call the committee together, and, if there is a quorum (a
majority of the committee, see § 43), he
should read, or have read, the entire resolutions referred to them; he should then
read each paragraph, and pause for amendments to be offered; when the amendments
to that paragraph are voted on he proceeds
to the next, only taking votes on amendments, as the committee cannot vote on the
adoption of matter referred to them by the
assembly.

If the committee originate the resolutions,
they vote, in the same way, on amendments
to each paragraph of the draft of the resolutions (which draft has been previously
prepared by one of their members or a sub-
committee) ; they do not vote on the separate paragraphs, but, having completed the
amendments, they vote on the adoption of
the entire report [see § 31]. When there is
a preamble it is considered last. If the report originates with the committee, all
amendments are to be incorporated in the
report; but if the resolutions were referred,
the committee cannot alter the text, but
must submit the original paper intact, with
their amendments (which may be in the

form of a substitute, § 23) written on a separate sheet.

A committee is a miniature assembly that must meet together in order to transact business, and usually one of its members should be appointed its clerk. Whatever is not agreed to by the majority of the members present at a meeting (at which a quorum, consisting of a majority of the members of the committee, shall be present) cannot form a part of its report. The minority may be permitted to submit their views in writing also, either together, or each member separately, but their reports can only be acted upon by voting to substitute one of them for the report of the committee [see § 30]. The rules of the assembly, as far as possible, shall apply in committee;* but a reconsideration [§ 27] of a vote shall be allowed, regardless of the time elapsed, only when every member who voted with the majority is present when the reconsideration is moved† A committee (except a

---

* The chairman of a committee usually takes the most active part in the discussion and work of the committee. A second is not required to a motion, nor, except in large committees, is one required to stand while speaking. In small committees motions may be dispensed with, but a vote should always be taken so as to know exactly what has been decided.

† Both the English common parliamentary law and

committee of the whole, § 32) may appoint
a sub-committee. When through with the
business assigned them, a motion is made
for the committee to "rise" (which is equivalent to the motion to adjourn), and that
the chairman (or some member who is more
familiar with the subject) make its report to
the assembly. The committee ceases to exist as soon as the assembly receives the report [§ 30], unless it is a standing committee.

The committee has no power to punish its
members for disorderly conduct, its resource
being to report the facts to the assembly.
No allusion can be made in the assembly to
what has occurred in committee, except it
be by a report of the committee, or by general consent. It is the duty of a committee
to meet on the call of any two of its members, if the chairman is absent or declines to
appoint such meeting. When a committee
adjourns without appointing a time for the
next meeting, it is called together in the

---

the rules of Congress prohibit the reconsideration of
a vote by a committee; but the strict enforcement of
this rule in ordinary committees would interfere with
rather than assist the transaction of business. The
rule given above seems more just, and more in accordance with the practice of ordinary committees, who
usually reconsider at pleasure. No improper advantage can be taken of the privilege, as long as every
member who voted with the majority must be present
when the reconsideration is moved.

same way as at its first meeting. When a committee adjourns to meet at another time, it is not necessary (though usually advisable) that absent members should be notified of the adjourned meeting.

29. Forms of Reports of Committees.

The form of a report is usually similar to the following:

A standing committee reports thus: "The committee on [insert name of committee] respectfully report" [or "beg leave to report," or "beg leave to submit the following report"], etc., letting the report follow.

A select or special committee reports as follows: "The committee to which was referred [state the matter referred] having considered the same, respectfully report," etc. Or for "The committee" is sometimes written "Your committee," or "The undersigned, a committee."

When a minority report is submitted, it should be in this form, the majority reporting as above): "The undersigned, a minority of a committee to which was referred," etc. The majority report is the report of the committee, and should never be made out as the report of the majority.

Reports sometimes conclude with, "All of which is respectfully submitted," but this is not necessary. They are sometimes signed only by the chairman of the committee, but if the matter is of much importance, it is better that the report be signed by every member who concurs. The report is not usually dated or addressed, but can be headed, as, for example, "Report of the Finance Committee of the Y. P. A., on Renting a Hall." The report of a committee should generally close or be accompanied with formal resolutions covering all its recommendations, so that the adopting of their report [§ 31] would have the effect to adopt all the resolutions necessary to carry out their recommendations.* The committee may be able to perform the entire duty assigned it by reporting a resolution, in which case the resolution alone is submitted in writing.

30. **Reception of Reports.** When the

* If the report of a committee were written in this form, "Your committee think the conduct of Mr. A. at the last meeting so disgraceful that they would recommend that he be expelled from the society," the adoption of the report would not have the effect to expel the member.

report of a committee is to be made, the chairman (or member appointed to make the report) informs the assembly that the committee to whom was referred such a subject or paper, has directed him to make a report thereon, or report it with or without amendment, as the case may be; either he or any other member may move that it be "received"* now or at some other specified time.

Usually the formality of a vote on the reception of a report of a committee is dispensed with, the time being settled by general consent. Should any one object, a formal motion becomes necessary. When the time arrives for the assembly to receive the

---

* A very common error is, after a report has been read, to move that it be received; whereas the fact that it has been read shows that it has been already received by the assembly. Another mistake, less common, but dangerous, is to vote that the report be accepted (which is equivalent to adopting it, see § 31), when the intention is only to have the report up for consideration and afterwards move its adoption. Still a third error is, to move that "the report be adopted and the committee be discharged," when the committee has reported in full and its report has been received, so that the committee has already ceased to exist. If the committee, however, has made but a partial report, or report progress, then it is in order to move that the committee be discharged from the further consideration of the subject.

† As soon as he has read the report it is well for him to move its acceptance [or adoption], or whatever motion is necessary to carry out the committee's recommendations.

report, the chairman of the committee reads it in his place† and then delivers it to the clerk, when it lies on the table till the assembly sees fit to consider it. If the report consists of a paper with amendments, the chairman of the committee reads the amendments with the coherence in the paper, explaining the alterations and the reasons of the committee for the amendments, till he has gone through the whole. If the report is very long it is not usually read until the assembly is ready to consider it [see § 31].

When the report has been received, whether it has been read or not, the committee is thereby dissolved, and can act no more unless it is revived by a vote to recommit. If the report is recommitted, all the parts of the report that have not been agreed to by the assembly are ignored by the committee as if the report had never been made.

If any member or members wish to submit a minority report (or reports) it is customary to receive it immediately after receiving the report of the committee; but it cannot be acted upon unless a motion is made to substitute it for the report of the committee.

31. Adoption of Reports.* When the assembly is to consider a report, if it has not been already done, a motion should be made to "adopt," "accept," or "agree to" the report, all of which, when carried, have the same effect, namely, to make the doings of the committee become the acts of the assembly, the same as if done by the assembly without the intervention of a committee, and therefore if the report contains formal resolutions it adopts those resolutions. While these motions are generally used indiscriminately, and all have the same effect, still it would probably be better to vary the motion according to the character of the report. Thus, if the report contains merely a statement of opinion or facts, the best form of the motion is to "accept the report;" if it also concludes with resolutions or orders, the motion would be more appropriately "to agree to the resolutions," or "to adopt the orders."† If either of these latter motions

---

* When the committee's report is only for the information of the assembly, it is not necessary to take any action on it after it has been read.

† "To adopt" the report is the most common of these motions in ordinary societies, and is used regardless of the character of the report. Its effect is generally understood, which is not the case with the motion to accept, as shown in the note to § 30 [which see for common errors in acting upon reports]. The last paragraph of § 29 shows how the form of the report influences the effect of its adoption.

is carried, the effect is to adopt the entire report of the committee.

After either of the above motions is made, the report is open to amendment,* and the matter stands before the assembly exactly the same as if there had been no committee, and the subject had been introduced by the motion of the member who made the report.

When a committee reports back a resolution which was referred to it, the question should be stated as follows: (a) If the committee recommends its adoption, or makes no recommendation, or recommends that it be not adopted, in either case the question should be on adopting the resolution. In the latter case it might be well to adopt a form similar to this: "The question is on the adoption of the resolution, the report of the committee to the contrary notwithstanding." (b) If the committee recommends that the resolution be indefinitely

---

* In the case of an annual report of an Executive Committee or Board of Managers which is published as their report, care should be taken in amending it to show clearly for what the Board is responsible and for what the Society. This can be done by prefixing to the report the statement that "The Report was adopted by the Society after striking out what is inclosed in brackets and adding what is printed in footnotes."

postponed, or postponed to a certain time,
the question should be on the indefinite postponement, or the postponement to the certain time.   (c) If the committee recommends that the resolution be amended in a
certain way, then the question should be on
the adoption of the proposed amendment to
the resolution, and then on adopting the
resolution.   In all these cases, immediately
after the committee's report is read, some
one should make the proper motion indicated above, and the proper person to make
it, if the committee makes any recommendation, is the member of the committee who
makes the report. If no motion is made,
the chairman may ask if some one will not
make such and such a motion, stating the
proper one, or he may state the question
without further delay, assuming the proper
motion to have been made. [See § 65, 1st
note.]

When a committee submits a report containing a number of paragraphs or sections,
as for instance a set of By-Laws, the whole
paper should be read through by either the
member reporting it, or the clerk, and the
reporting member, or some one else, should
move its adoption, unless this has been previously done. The chairman having stated

the question on the adoption of the report,
he should direct the member who reported
it, or the clerk, to read the first paragraph,*
and when it has been read, inquire, "Are
there any amendments proposed to this paragraph?" He should then pause for any remarks or amendments, always giving the
preference to the member who submitted
the report if he wishes the floor. When
satisfied no one else desires the floor, he
should say, "No amendments (or no further
amendments) being offered to this paragraph, the next will be read." In this way
each paragraph is read and amended, when
the chair states that the entire report, or all

---

* By "paragraphs" is meant in this rule the separate divisions of the proposition, and they may be
Articles, Sections, Paragraphs, or separate resolutions.

No vote should be taken on the adoption of the
several paragraphs, one vote being taken finally on
the adoption of the whole paper. By not adopting
separately the different paragraphs, it is in order,
after they have all been amended, to go back and
amend any of them still further. In committee a
similar paper would be treated the same way [see
§ 28]. In § 48 (b) an illustration is given of the
practical application of this section.

If each paragraph or section is adopted separately.
it is improper afterwards to vote on the adoption of
the whole report. as this would be voting to adopt
what has been already adopted in detail. So, too, it
is out of order to go back and amend a paragraph
that has been adopted, until after it has been reconsidered.

of the resolutions, have been read and are
open to amendment. At this stage new
paragraphs may be inserted, or even those
originally in the report may be further
amended, as they have not yet been adopted.
If there is a preamble it should be read and
amended after the body of the resolutions
has been perfected, and then a vote is taken
on adopting the entire report as amended.

When a committee reports back a paper
with amendments, the reporting member
reads only the amendments and then moves
their adoption. The chairman, after stating
the question on the adoption of the amendments, calls for the reading of the first
amendment, after which it is open for debate and amendment. A vote is then taken
on adopting this amendment, and the next
is read, and so on till the amendments are
adopted or rejected, admitting amendments
to the committee's amendments, but no others. When through with the committee's
amendments, the chairman pauses for any
other amendments to be proposed by the
assembly; and when these are voted on he
puts the question on agreeing to, or adopting, the paper as amended, unless in a case
like revising the By-Laws, where they have
been already adopted. By "suspending the

rules" [§ 18], or by general consent, a report can be at once adopted without following any of the above routine. [See § 34 for the privileges in debate of the member making the report.]

32. Committee of the Whole. When an assembly has to consider a subject which it does not wish to refer to a committee, and yet where the subject matter is not well digested and put into proper form for its definite action, or when, for any other reason, it is desirable for the assembly to consider a subject with all the freedom of an ordinary committee, it is the practice to refer the matter to the "Committee of the Whole."* If it is desired to consider the question at once, the motion is made, "That the assembly do now resolve itself into a committee of the whole, to take under consideration," etc., specifying the subject. This is really a motion to "commit." [See § 22 for its order of precedence, etc.] If adopted, the

---

* In large assemblies, such as the U. S. House of Representatives, where a member can speak to any question but once, the committee of the whole seems almost a necessity, as it allows the freest discussion of a subject, while at any time it can rise and thus bring into force the strict rules of the assembly.

chairman immediately calls another member to the chair, and takes his place as a member of the committee. The committee is under the rules of the assembly, excepting as stated hereafter in this section.

The only motions in order are to amend and adopt, and that the committee "rise and report," as it cannot adjourn; nor can it order the "yeas and nays" [§ 38]. The only way to close or limit debate in committee of the whole is for the assembly to vote that the debate in committee shall cease at a certain time, or that after a certain time no debate shall be allowed, excepting on new amendments, and then only one speech in favor of and one against it, of say five minutes each; or in some other way regulate the time for debate.*

If no limit is prescribed, any member may

---

* In Congress no motion to limit debate in committee of the whole is in order till after the subject has been already considered in committee of the whole. As no subject would probably be considered more than once in committee of the whole, in an ordinary society, the enforcement of this rule would practically prevent such a society from putting any limit to debate in the committee. The rule, as given above, allows the society, whenever resolving itself into committee of the whole, to impose upon the debate in the committee such restrictions as are allowed in Congress after the subject has already been considered in committee of the whole.

speak as often as he can get the floor, and
as long each time as is allowed in debate in
the assembly, provided no one wishes the
floor who has not spoken on that particular
question.   Debate having been closed at a
particular time by order of the assembly, it
is not competent for the committee, even by
unanimous consent, to extend the time. The
committee cannot refer the subject to another committee.   Like other committees
[§ 28], it cannot alter the text of any resolution referred to it; but if the resolution
originated in the committee, then all the
amendments are incorporated in it.

When it is through with the consideration of the subject referred to it, or if it
wishes to adjourn, or to have the assembly
limit debate, a motion is made that "the
committee rise and report," etc., specifying
the result of its proceedings.   This motion
"to rise" is equivalent to the motion to adjourn in the assembly, and is always in order (except when another member has the
floor), and is undebatable.   As soon as this
motion is adopted the presiding officer takes
the chair, and the chairman of the committee, having resumed his place in the assembly, rises and informs him that "the committee has gone through the business re-

ferred to it, and that he is ready to make the report when the assembly is ready to receive it;" or he will make such other report as will suit the case.

The clerk does not record the proceedings of the committee on the minutes, but should keep a memorandum of the proceedings for the use of the committee. In large assemblies the clerk vacates his chair, which is occupied by the chairman of the committee, and the assistant clerk acts as clerk of the committee. Should the committee get disorderly, and the chairman be unable to preserve order, the presiding officer can take the chair, and declare the committee dissolved. The quorum of the committee of the whole is the same as that of the assembly [§ 43]. If the committee finds itself without a quorum, it can only rise and report the fact to the assembly, which in such a case would have to adjourn.

33. Informal Consideration of a Question (or acting *as if in committee of the whole*).

It has become customary in many assemblies, instead of going into committee of the whole, to consider the question "informally," and afterwards to act "formally." In a small assembly there is no objection to this.* While acting informally upon any resolutions, the assembly can only amend and adopt them, and without further motion the chairman announces that "the assembly, acting informally [or as in committee of the whole], has had such subject under consideration, and has made certain amendments, which he will report." The subject comes before the assembly then as if reported by a committee. While acting informally the chairman retains his seat, as it is not necessary to move that the committee rise; but at any time the adoption of such motions as to adjourn, the previous question, to commit, or any motion except to amend or adopt, puts an end to the informal consideration; as, for example, the motion to commit is equivalent to the following motions when in committee of the whole: (1)

---

* In the U. S. Senate all bills, joint resolutions and treaties, upon their second reading are considered "as if the Senate were in committee of the whole," which is equivalent to considering them informally. [U. S. Senate Rules, 28 and 38.] In large assemblies it is better to follow the practice of the House of Representatives, and go into committee of the whole.

That the committee rise; (2) that the committee of the whole be discharged from the further consideration of the subject; and (3) that it be referred to a committee.

While acting informally, every member can speak as many times as he pleases, and as long each time as permitted in the assembly [§ 34], and the informal action may be rejected or altered by the assembly. While the clerk should keep a memorandum of the informal proceedings, it should not be entered on the minutes, being only for temporary use. The chairman's report to the assembly of the informal action should be entered on the minutes, as it belongs to the assembly's proceedings.

Art. V. Debate and Decorum.
[§§ 34-37.]

34. Debate.* When a motion is made and seconded, it shall be stated by the chairman before being debated [see § 3]. When any member is about to speak in debate he shall rise and respectfully address himself to "Mr. Chairman." ["Mr. President" is

---

* In connection with this section read §§ 1-5.

used where that is the designated title of
the presiding officer; "Mr. Moderator"* is
more common in religious meetings. In every case the presiding officer should be addressed by his official title.] The chairman
shall then announce his name. By parliamentary courtesy,† the member upon whose
motion a subject is brought before the assembly is first entitled to the floor [see §
2], even though another member has risen
first and addressed the chair [in case of a
report of a committee it is the member who
presents the report]; and he is also entitled
to close the debate, but not until every
member choosing to speak has spoken.
When a member reports a measure from a
committee, he cannot in any way be deprived of his right to close the debate; so
if the previous question [§ 20 is ordered the
chairman at once assigns him the floor to
close the debate. With this exception, no
member shall speak more than twice to the

---

* "Brother Moderator" is more commonly used in
some sections of the country; but in strictness of
speech it implies an official equality between the
speaker and the chairman that does not exist, or in
other words it implies that they are both moderators.
If a woman is in the chair, the only change in the
address is by substituting "Mrs." or "Miss," as the
case may be, or "Madam," for "Mr." Thus, "Mrs.
President."

† The U. S. House of Representatives provides for
this by rule.

same question (only once to a question of order § 14), nor longer than ten minutes at one time, without leave of the assembly, and the question upon granting the leave shall be decided by a two-thirds vote [§ 39] without debate.* If greater freedom is desired, the proper course is to refer the subject to the committee of the whole [§ 32], or to consider it informally [§ 33]. [For limiting or closing the debate see § 37.]

No member can speak the second time to a question until every member choosing to speak has spoken. But an amendment, or any other motion, being offered, makes the real question before the assembly a different one, and, in regard to the right to debate, is treated as a new question. Merely asking a question, or making a suggestion, is not considered as speaking. The maker of a motion,

---

* The limit in time should vary to suit circumstances, but the limit of two speeches of ten minutes each will usually answer in ordinary assemblies, and when desirable, by a two-thirds vote it can be increased, as shown above, or diminished as shown in § 37. In the U. S. House of Representatives no member can speak more than once to the same question, nor longer than one hour. The fourth rule of the Senate is as follows: "No senator shall speak more than twice in any one debate, on the same day, without leave of the Senate, which question shall be decided without debate." If no rule is adopted, each member can speak but once to the same question.

though he can vote against it, cannot speak against his own motion.

When an amendment is pending the debate must be confined to the merits of the amendment, unless it is of such a nature that its decision practically decides the main question.

The chairman cannot close the debate as long as any member desires to speak, and should a member claim the floor after the chairman has risen to put the question, or even after the affirmative vote has been taken, provided the negative has not been put, he has a right to resume the debate or make a motion.

35. Undebatable Questions and those Opening the Main Question to Debate. The following questions shall be decided without debate, all others being debatable [see note at end of this section]:

To *Fix the Time to which the Assembly shall Adjourn* (when a privileged question, § 10).

To *Adjourn* [§ 11], (or in committee, *to rise*, which is used instead of to adjourn).

For the *Orders of the Day* [§ 13], and questions relating to the *priority of business*.

An *Appeal* [§ 14], when made while the Previous Question is pending, or when simply relating to indecorum or transgressions of the rules of speaking, or to the priority of business.

Objection to the Consideration of a Question [§ 15].

To *Lay on the Table,* or to *Take from the Table* [§ 19].

The *Previous Question* [§ 20].

To *Reconsider* [§ 27] a question which is itself undebatable.

Questions relating to *Reading of Papers* [§ 16], or *Withdrawing a Motion* [§ 17], or *Suspending the Rules* [§ 18], or *extending the limits of debate* [§ 34], or *limiting or closing debate* [§ 37], or granting *leave to continue his speech* to one who has been guilty of indecorum in debate [§ 36].

The motion *to postpone to a certain time,* [§ 21] allows of but very limited debate, which must be confined to the propriety of the postponement. . When an *amendment* is before the assembly the main question cannot be debated excepting so far as it is necessarily involved in the amendment. But the following motions open to discussion the entire merits of the main question:

To Commit [§ 22].
To Postpone Indefinitely [§ 24].
To Rescind [§ 25].
To Reconsider a debatable question [§ 27].

The distinction between debate and making suggestions or asking a question should always be kept in view, and, when the latter will assist the assembly in determining the question, is allowed, to a limited extent, even though the question before the assembly is undebatable.

NOTE ON UNDEBATABLE QUESTIONS.—The English common parliamentary law makes all motions debatable, unless there is a rule adopted limiting debate; but every assembly is obliged to restrict debate upon certain motions. The restrictions to debate prescribed in this section conform to the practice of Congress, where, however, it is very common to allow of brief remarks upon the most undebatable questions, sometimes five or six members speaking. This, of course, is allowed only when no one objects.

By examining the above list it will be found that, while free debate is allowed upon every principal question [§ 6], it is permitted or prohibited upon other questions in accordance with the following principles:

(*a*) Highly privileged questions, as a rule, should not be debated, as in that case they could be used to prevent the assembly from coming to a vote on the main question (for instance, if the motion to adjourn were debatable, it could be used [see § 11] in a way to greatly hinder business). *High privilege is, as a rule, incompatible with the right of debate on the privileged question.*

(*b*) A motion that has the effect to suppress a question before the assembly, so that it cannot again be taken up that session [§ 42], allows of free debate; and a Subsidiary Motion [§ 7, except Commit, which see below], is debatable to just the extent that it interferes with the right of the assembly to take up the original question at its pleasure.

Illustrations: To "Indefinitely Postpone" [§ 24] a question places it out of the power of the assembly to again take it up during that session, and consequently this motion allows of free debate, even involving the whole merits of the original question.

To "Postpone to a certain time" prevents the assembly taking up the question till the specified time, and therefore allows of limited debate upon the propriety of the postponement.

To "Lay on the Table" leaves the question so that the assembly can at any time consider it, and therefore should not be, and is not debatable.*

To "Commit" would not be very debatable, according to this rule, but it is an exception, because it is often important that the committee should know the views of the assembly on the question, and it therefore is not only debatable, but opens to debate the whole question which it is proposed to refer to the committee.

36. Decorum in Debate [see § 2]. In debate a member must confine himself to the question before the assembly, and avoid personalities. He cannot reflect upon any act of the assembly, unless he intends to conclude his remarks with a motion to rescind

---

* See Note at close of § 19 for abuses of this motion.

such action or else while debating such motion. In referring to another member, he should, as much as possible, avoid using his name, rather referring to him as "the member who spoke last," or in some other way describing him. The officers of the assembly should always be referred to by their official titles. It is not allowable to arraign the motives of a member, but the nature or consequences of a measure may be condemned in strong terms. It is not the man, but the measure, that is the subject of debate. If at any time the chairman rises to state a point of order, or give information, or otherwise speak, within his privilege [see § 40], the member speaking must take his seat till the chairman has been first heard. When called to order, the member must sit down until the question of order is decided. If his remarks are decided to be improper, he cannot proceed, if any one objects, without the leave of the assembly expressed by a vote, upon which question there shall be no debate.

Disorderly words should be taken down by the member who objects to them, or by the clerk, and then read to the member; if he denies them, the assembly shall decide by

a vote whether they are his words or not.
If a member cannot justify the words he
used, and will not suitably apologize for
using them, it is the duty of the assembly to
act in the case.   If the disorderly words are
of a personal nature, before the assembly
proceeds to deliberate upon the case both
parties to the personality should retire, it being a general rule that no member should
be present in the assembly when any matter
relating to himself is under debate.   It is
not, however, necessary for the member ob-
jecting to the words to retire unless he is
personally involved in the case. If any business has taken place since the member
spoke, it is too late to take notice of any
disorderly words he used.

During debate, and while the chairman is
speaking, or the assembly is engaged in voting, no member is permitted to disturb the
assembly by whispering, or walking across
the floor, or in any other way.

37.   **Closing Debate.**   Debate upon a
question is not closed by the chairman rising to put the question, as, until both the affirmative and negative are put, a member
can claim the floor, and reopen debate [see

§ 38]. Debate can be closed by the following motions,* which are undebatable [§ 35], and, except to Lay on the Table, shall require a two-thirds† vote for their adoption [§ 39] :

(*a*) *An Objection to the Consideration of a Question* [§ 15], which is allowable only when the question is first introduced, and if sustained, not only stops debate, but also throws the subject out of the assembly for that session [§ 42] ; which latter effect is the one for which it was designed.

(*b*) To *Lay on the Table* [§ 19], which, if adopted, carries the question to the table, from which it cannot be taken unless a majority favor such action.

(*c*) The *Previous Question* [§ 20],

---

* It will be noticed that the first two of these motions only close debate by virtue of their suppressing the question itself. The circumstances under which each of these motions to suppress debate and to suppress the question should be used, are explained in §§ 58, 59.

† In the U. S. House of Representatives, where each speaker can occupy the floor one hour, any of these motions to cut off debate can be adopted by a mere majority, but practically they are not used until after some debate: Rule 28, ¶ 3, H. R., expressly provides that forty minutes, twenty on each side, shall be allowed for debate whenever the previous question is ordered on a proposition on which there has been no debate, or when the rules are suspended. In ordinary societies harmony is so essential that a two-thirds vote should be required to force the assembly to a final vote without allowing free debate [see note to § 39].

which, if adopted, cuts off debate, and brings the assembly to a vote on the pending question only, excepting where the pending motion is an amendment or a motion to commit, when it also applies to the question to be amended or committed, unless it is demanded only on the amendment or the motion to commit. When it is ordered on an amendment, or an amendment of an amendment, debate is closed and the vote taken on the amendment, when the effect of the previous question is then exhausted, and new amendments can be offered and debated.

(*d*) For the assembly to adopt an *order* (1) *limiting debate* upon a special subject, either as to the number or length of the speeches; or (2) *closing debate* upon the subject at a stated time, when all pending questions shall be put to vote without further debate. Either of these two measures may be applied simply to a pending amendment, or an amendment thereto; and when this is voted upon, the original question is still open to debate and amendment.

Art. VI. Vote.

[§§ 38, 39.]

38. Voting. Whenever from the nature of the question it permits of no modification or debate, the chairman immediately puts it to vote; if the question is debatable, when the chairman thinks the debate has been brought to a close he should inquire if the assembly is ready for the question, and if no one rises he puts the question to vote. There are various forms for putting the question in use in different parts of the country. The rule in Congress, in the House of Representatives, requires questions to be put as follows: "As many as are in favor [as the question may be] say *aye;*" and after the affirmative voice is expressed, "As many as are opposed say *no.*" The following form is very common: "It has been moved and seconded that [here state the question]; as many as are in favor of the motion say *aye;* those opposed *no.*" Or, if the motion is for the adoption of a certain resolution, after it has been read the chairman can say, "You have heard the resolution read; those in favor of its adoption will hold up the right hand; those opposed will manifest it by the same sign." These examples* are sufficient to show the usual methods of putting a question, the affirmative being always put first.

A majority vote, that is, a majority of the votes cast, ignoring blanks, is sufficient for the adoption of any motion that is in order, except those mentioned in § 39, which require a two-thirds vote. A plurality vote never adopts a motion nor elects any one except by virtue of a special rule previously adopted. [§ 39, 1st note.]

When a vote is taken the chairman should always announce the result in the following form: "The motion is carried—the resolution is adopted," or, "The ayes have it—the resolution is adopted." If, when he announces a vote, any member rises and states that he doubts the vote, or calls for a "division," the chairman shall say, "A division is called for; those in favor of the motion will rise." After counting these, and announcing the number, he shall say, "Those opposed will rise." He will count these, an-

---

* See § 65 and also the Table of Rules, p. 10, for the forms of stating and putting certain questions.

nounce the number, and declare the result; that is, whether the motion is carried or lost. Instead of counting the vote himself, he can direct the secretary, or appoint tellers, to make the count and report to him. When tellers are appointed, they should be selected from both sides of the question. A member has the right to change his vote (when not made by ballot) before the decision of the question has been finally and conclusively pronounced by the chair, but not afterwards.

Until the negative is put, it is in order for any member, in the same manner as if the voting had not been commenced, to rise and speak, make motions for amendment or otherwise, and thus renew the debate; and this, whether the member was in the assembly room or not when the question was put and the vote partly taken. After the chairman has announced the vote, if it is found that a member has risen and addressed the chair before the negative had been put, he is entitled to be heard on the question, the same as though the vote had not been taken. In such cases the question is in the same condition as if it had never been put.

No one can vote on a question affecting himself; but if more than one name is included in the resolution (though a sense of delicacy would prevent this right being exercised, excepting when it would change the vote) all are entitled to vote; for if this were not so, a minority could control an assembly by including the names of a sufficient number in a motion, say for preferring charges against them, and suspend them, or even expel them from the assembly.*

When there is a tie vote the motion fails, unless the chairman gives his vote for the affirmative, which he is at liberty to do, as he has a right to vote whenever his vote will affect the result. Where his vote in the negative will make a tie, he can cast it and thus defeat the measure [§ 40]. In case of an Appeal [§ 14], though the question is, "Shall the decision of the chair stand as the judgment of the assembly?" a tie vote sustains the chair, upon the principle that the decision of the chair can only be reversed by a majority.

---

* But, after charges are preferred against a member, and the assembly has ordered him to appear for trial, he is theoretically in arrest, and is deprived of all rights of membership until his case is disposed of.

Another form of voting is by *ballot*. This method is adopted only when required by the constitution or by-laws of the assembly, or when the assembly has ordered the vote to be so taken. The chairman, in such cases, appoints at least two tellers, who distribute slips of paper, upon which each member, including the chairman, writes his vote.* In voting by ballot members are not restricted to persons who have been nominated. Closing nominations prevents the public indorsement of any other candidates, but does not prevent their being voted for and being elected. When the votes are collected, they are counted by the tellers, and the result reported to the chairman, who announces it to the assembly. The chairman announces the result of the vote, in case of an election to office, in a manner similar to the following: "The whole number of votes cast is —; the number necessary for an election is —; Mr. A received —; Mr. B, —; Mr. C, —. Mr. B, having received the required number, is

---

* Should the chairman neglect to vote before the ballots are counted, he cannot then vote without the permission of the assembly. In ordinary assemblies ballots should be credited to the candidates for whom they were intended, whenever that can be determined, regardless of inaccuracies in writing them.

elected——." Where there is only one candi-
date for an office, and the constitution requires the vote to be by ballot, it is common
to authorize the clerk to cast the vote of the
assembly for such and such a person; if
anyone objects, however, it is necessary to
ballot in the usual way.* So, when a motion is made to make a vote unanimous, it
fails if anyone objects. In counting the
ballots all blanks are ignored.

The assembly can, by a majority vote, order that the vote on any question be taken
by *Yeas and Nays.*‡ In this method of

---

* It should always be remembered that this can be
done only by unanimous consent, and it is doubtful
whether it should ever be allowed. An election, like
every other vote of the assembly, takes effect immediately unless there is a rule to the contrary.

† Taking a vote by yeas and nays, which has the
effect to place on the record how each member votes,
is peculiar to this country, and, while it consumes a
great deal of time, is rarely useful in ordinary societies. While it can never be used to hinder business,
as long as the above rule is observed, it should not be
used at all in a mass meeting, or in any other assembly whose members are not responsible to a con-
stituency. By the Constitution, one-fifth of the members present can, in either house of Congress, order
a vote to be taken by yeas and nays, and. to avoid
some of the resulting inconveniences, Congress has
required, for instance, that the previous question shall
be seconded by a majority, thus avoiding the yeas and
nays until a majority are in favor of ordering the
main question. In representative bodies this method
of voting is very useful, especially where the proceedings are published, as it enables the people to know
how their representatives voted on important measures. If there is no legal or constitutional provision

voting the chairman states both sides of the question at once; the clerk calls the roll, and each member, as his name is called, rises and answers *yes* or *no,* and the clerk notes his answer. Upon the completion of the roll-call the clerk reads over the names of those who answered in the affirmative, and afterwards those in the negative, that mistakes may be corrected; he then gives the number voting on each side to the chairman, who announces the result. An entry must be made in the minutes of the names of all voting in the affirmative, and also of those in the negative.

The form of putting a question upon which the vote has been ordered to be taken by yeas and nays is similar to the following: "As many as are in favor of the adoption of these resolutions will, when their names are called, answer *yes* [or *aye*] ; those opposed will answer *no.*" The chairman will then direct the clerk to call the roll. The nega-

---

for the yeas and nays being ordered by a minority in a representative body, they should adopt a rule allowing the yeas and nays to be ordered by a one-fifth vote, as in Congress, or even by a much smaller number. In some small bodies a vote on a resolution must be taken by yeas and nays, upon the demand of a single member.

tive being put at the same time as the affirmative, it is too late, after one person has
answered to the roll-call, to renew the debate. After the commencement of the roll-
call it is too late to ask to be excused from
voting. The yeas and nays cannot be ordered in committee of the whole [§ 32].

**39. Motions Requiring More than a
Majority Vote.*** The following motions
shall require a two-thirds vote for their
adoption, all others requiring a majority, as
the right of discussion, and the right to
have the rules enforced, should not be
abridged by a mere majority:

---

* A two-thirds, or majority, vote means two-thirds
or a majority of votes cast, ignoring blanks, which
should never be counted. Sometimes By-Laws provide
for a vote of two-thirds of the members present, or
simply of two-thirds of the members, which may be
very different from a two-thirds vote. Thus, if twelve
members vote on a question in a meeting of a society
where twenty are present out of a total membership
of thirty, a two-thirds vote would be eight ; a two-
thirds vote of those present would be fourteen ; and a
vote of two-thirds of the members would be twenty.
In this case a majority vote would be seven.

A person is said to have a *plurality* vote when he
has more votes for a certain office or position than
any of his rivals. In civil government, as a rule all
officers elected by a popular vote are elected by a
plurality. But in a deliberative assembly, where voting may be repeated until there is an election, a plurality never elects except by virtue of a special rule.

To Amend the Rules (requires pre-
    vious notice also)................See § 45
To Suspend the Rules............   "   § 18
To Make a Special Order........   "   § 13
*To Take up a Question out of its
    Proper Order* ....   "   § 13
*An Objection to the Consideration of
    a Question** ....   "   § 15
To Extend the Limits of Debate....   "   § 34
To Close or Limit Debate...........   "   § 37
The Previous Question.............   "   § 20

Note on Motions Requiring More Than a
Majority Vote.—Every motion in this list has
the effect to suspend or change some rule or custom of deliberative bodies. Judging from their
form, this would be true of only the first two,
but a closer examination will show that the others have a similar effect.

To make a special order suspends all the rules
that interfere with the consideration of the question at the specified time.

To take up a question out of its proper order
is a change in the order of business.

An objection to the consideration of a question,
if sustained, suspends or conflicts with the right
of a member to introduce a measure to the assembly; a right which certainly has been established by custom, if it is not inherent to the very
idea of a deliberative body. [Though Rule 41
H. R. allows a majority vote to decide this question, it is so inexpedient that the rule has not
been taken advantage of lately.]

To extend the limits of debate, is to suspend
a rule or an order of the assembly.

---

* The negative vote on considering the question
must be two-thirds to dismiss the question for that
session.

The Previous Question, and motions to *close or limit debate,* have the effect of forcing the assembly to take final action upon a question without allowing discussion; in other words, they suspend this fundamental principle of deliberative bodies, namely, that the assembly shall not be forced to final action on a question until every member has had an opportunity of discussing its merits. The very idea of a deliberative assembly is that it is a body to deliberate upon questions, and therefore members must have the right of introducing questions, and of discussing their merits, before expressing their deliberate sense upon them. [Of course, a majority can lay the question on the table, and thus stop debate; but in this case the assembly can at any time take it from the table. By this means the majority can instantly get rid of any question until they wish to consider it.]

But there are times when it is expedient to suspend these rights to introduce and debate questions, just the same as it is frequently an advantage to suspend the rules of the assembly, or to change the order of business. If, however, a bare majority could at any time suspend or change these rules and privileges, they would be of but little value. Experience has shown that a two-thirds vote should be required to adopt any motion that has the effect to suspend or change the rules or established order of business, and the rule above is made on this general principle. [The old parliamentary practice did not allow of a suspension of the rules except by unanimous consent.]

As just stated, Congress, by rule, allows a majority to sustain an objection to the consideration of a question, but the rule has very properly gone out of use. So, too, the previous question, and motions to close or limit debate, while not used in the Senate, can be adopted by a majority in the House of Representatives.

On account of the immense amount of business to be transacted during each session by the National House of Representatives, and the large number of members each one of whom is entitled to the floor in debate for one hour, it seems an absolute necessity for them to permit a majority to limit or cut off entirely the debate, and thus practically to suspend one of the fundamental rules of deliberative bodies. This is the more necessary in Congress because the party lines are strictly drawn, and the minority could almost stop legislation if they could prevent the debate from being cut off.

In all bodies situated in these respects like Congress, a rule should be adopted allowing a majority to adopt the previous question, and motions to limit or close debate. [See the last note to § 38 in reference to the yeas and nays being ordered by a one-fifth vote in Congress, and by even a smaller vote in some other bodies. The two notes in the Introduction, on pp. 19-21, may be read with advantage in connection with this note.]

Art. VII. The Officers and the Minutes.

[§§ 40, 41.]

40. Chairman* or President. The presiding officer, when no special title has been assigned him, is ordinarily called the Chair-

---

* In connection with this section read §§ 2, 24, 44, 65.

man (or in religious assemblies more usually the Moderator) ; frequently the constitution of the assembly prescribes for him a title, such as President.

His duties are generally as follows:

To open the session at the time at which the assembly is to meet, by taking the chair and calling the members to order; to announce the business before the assembly in the order in which it is to be acted upon [§ 44] ; to state and to put to vote [§§ 38, 65] all questions which are regularly moved, or necessarily arise in the course of proceedings, and to announce the result of the vote;

To restrain the members, when engaged in debate, within the rules of order;*• to enforce on all occasions the observance of order and decorum [§ 36] among the members, deciding all questions of order (subject to an appeal to the assembly by any two members, § 14), and to inform the assembly when necessary, or when referred to for the purpose, on a point of order or practice.

To authenticate, by his signature, when necessary, all the acts, orders, and proceedings of the assembly, and in general to rep-

*Should the disorder become so great that business cannot be transacted, and the chairman cannot enforce order, as a last resort he can declare the assembly adjourned.

resent and stand for the assembly, declaring its will, and in all things obeying its commands.

The chairman shall rise† to put a question to vote, but may state it sitting; he shall also rise from his seat (without calling any one to the chair) when speaking to a question of order, which he can do in preference to other members. In referring to himself he should always use his official title, thus: "The chair decides so and so," not "I decide, etc." When a member has the floor, the chairman cannot interrupt him so long as he does not transgress any of the rules of the assembly, excepting as provided in § 2.

He is entitled to vote when the vote is by ballot,* and in all other cases where the vote would change the result. Thus, in a case where a two-thirds vote is necessary, and his vote thrown with the minority would prevent the adoption of the question, he can cast his vote; so, also, he can vote with the minority when it will produce a tie vote and thus cause the motion to fail. Whenever a motion is made referring es-

---

† It is not customary for the chairman to rise while putting questions in very small bodies, such as committees, boards of trustees, etc.

* But this right is lost if he does not use it before the tellers have commenced to count the ballots. The assembly can give leave to the chairman to vote under such circumstances.

pecially to the chairman, the secretary, or,
on his failure to do so, the maker of the
motion, should put it to vote.

The chairman can, if it is necessary to va-
cate the chair, appoint a chairman *pro
tem.*,* but the first adjournment puts an end
to the appointment, which the assembly can
terminate before, if it pleases, by electing
another chairman. But the regular chairman, knowing that he will be absent from a
future meeting, cannot authorize another
member to act in his place at such meeting;
the clerk [§ 41], or, in his absence, any
member should, in such case, call the meeting to order, and a chairman *pro tem.* be
elected who would hold office during that
session [§ 42], unless such office was terminated by the entrance of the regular chairman. If there are vice-presidents, the first
on the list that is present takes the chair
during the absence of the president.

The chairman sometimes calls a member
to the chair, and himself takes part in the
debate; but this should rarely be done, and
nothing can justify it in a case where much
feeling is shown, and there is a liability to
difficulty in preserving order. If the chair-

---

* When there are vice-presidents, then the first one
on the list that is present is, by virtue of his office,
chairman during the absence of the president, and
should always be called to the chair when the president temporarily vacates it.

man has even the appearance of being a partisan, he loses much of his ability to control those who are on the opposite side of the question.*

The chairman should not only be familiar with parliamentary usage, and set the example of strict conformity thereto,† but he

---

* See § 28 for duties of Chairmen of Committees.
The unfortunate habit many chairmen have of constantly speaking on questions before the assembly, even interrupting the member who has the floor, is unjustified by either the common parliamentary law or the practice of Congress. One who expects to take an active part in debate should never accept the chair.

"It is a general rule in all deliberative assemblies, that the presiding officer shall not participate in the debate, or other proceedings, in any other capacity than as such officer. He is only allowed, therefore, to state matters of fact within his knowledge; to inform the assembly on points of order or the course of proceeding, when called upon for that purpose, or when he finds it necessary to do so; and, on appeals from his decision on question of order, to address the assembly in debate." [Cushing's Manual, § 202.]

"Though the Speaker [Chairman] may of right speak to matters of order and be first heard, he is restrained from speaking on any other subject except where the assembly have occasion for facts within his knowledge; then he may, with their leave, state the matter of fact." [Jefferson's Manual, sec. xvii, and Barclay's "Digest of the Rules and Practice of the House of Representatives U. S," page 195.]

† No rules will take the place of tact and common sense on the part of the chairman. While usually he need not wait for motions of routine, or for a motion to be seconded when he knows it is favored by others [see first note to § 65], yet if this is objected to, it is safer instantly to require the forms of parliamentary law to be observed. By general consent many things can be done that will save much time, but where the assembly is very large, or is divided and contains members who are continually raising points of order, the most expeditious and safe course is to

should be a man of executive ability, capable of controlling men; and it should never be forgotten, that, to control others, it is necessary to control one's self. An excited chairman can scarcely fail to cause trouble in a meeting.

A chairman should not permit the object of a meeting to be defeated by a few factious persons using parliamentary forms with the evident object of obstructing business. In such a case he should refuse to entertain the dilatory motion, and, if an appeal is taken, he should entertain it, and, if sustained by a large majority, he can afterwards refuse to entertain even an appeal made by the faction, while they are continuing their obstruction. But the chair should never adopt such a course merely to expe-

---

enforce strictly all the rules and forms of parliamentary law.

Whenever an improper motion is made, instead of simply ruling it out of order, it is well for the chairman to suggest how the desired object can be accomplished. Thus, if it is moved "to postpone the question," he should say that if the time is not specified the proper motion is "that the question lie on the table." So, if it were moved "to lay the question on the table until a certain time," he should suggest that the proper motion is "to postpone the question to that time." Or, if it were moved to reject a resolution, he should say, "the question is on indefinitely postponing the resolution," as that is the parliamentary form of the question.

For "Hints to Inexperienced Chairmen," see § 50.

dite business, when the opposition is not factious. It is only justifiable when it is perfectly clear that the opposition is trying to obstruct business.

A chairman will often find himself perplexed with the difficulties attending his position, and in such cases he will do well to heed the advice of a distinguished writer on parliamentary law, and recollect that

"The great purpose of all rules and forms is to subserve the will of the assembly rather than to restrain it; to facilitate, and not to obstruct, the expression of their deliberate sense."

41. Clerk or Secretary *and the Minutes.* The recording officer is usually called the "Clerk" or "Secretary,"* and the record of proceedings the "Minutes." His desk should be near that of the chairman and in the absence of the chairman (if there is no vice-president present), when the hour for

---

* When there are two secretaries, he is termed the "recording secretary," and the other one the "corresponding secretary." In many societies the secretary, besides acting as recording officer, collects the dues of members, and thus becomes to a certain extent a financial officer. In most cases the treasurer acts as banker, only paying on the order of the society, signed by the secretary alone, or by the president and secretary. In such cases the secretary becomes in reality the financial officer of the society, and should make reports to the society of funds received and from what sources, and of the funds expended and for what purposes. See § 52 for his duties as financial officer.

opening the session arrives, it is his duty to
call the meeting to order, and to preside until the election of a chairman *pro tem.*,
which should be done immediately. He
should keep a record of the proceedings,
commencing in a form similar to the following:* "At a regular quarterly meeting
of [state the name of the society], held on
the 31st day of March, 1875, at [state the
place of meeting], the president in the
chair, the minutes were read by the clerk
and approved." If the regular clerk is absent, insert after the words "in the chair"
the following: "The clerk being absent,
Robert Smith was appointed clerk *pro tem.*
The minutes were then read and approved."
If the minutes were not read, say "The
reading of the minutes was dispensed
with." The above form will show the es-
sentials, which are as follows: (*a*) The
kind of meeting, "regular" [or stated] or
"special," or "adjourned regular" or "adjourned special;" (*b*) name of the assembly; (*c*) date and place of meeting (excepting when the place is always the same);
(*d*) the fact of the presence of the regular
chairman and clerk, or in their absence the
names of their substitutes; (*e*) whether the

* See Clerk and Minutes, in Part II, § 51.

minutes of the previous meeting were approved.

The minutes should be neatly written with ink in the record book, leaving a margin for corrections, and taken to the meetings of the society so as to be read for corrections, and approval.* After approval, however, without a reconsideration, it is in order at any future time for the society to further correct them, regardless of the time that has elapsed and the number of times they have already been amended.

The minutes should be signed by the person who acted as clerk for that meeting; in some societies the chairman must also sign them. When published, they should be signed by both officers.

In keeping the minutes, much depends upon the kind of meeting, and whether the minutes are to be published. Under no circumstances, however, should the clerk criti-

---

* In many organizations it is preferable for the secretary to keep his original pencil notes in a pocket memorandum book which he carries to every meeting, and these original notes, as corrected, are approved and then copied into the permanent records. This plan results usually in neater records, but the original notes should be kept until they are carefully compared with the permanent records.

cize in the minutes, either favorably or otherwise, anything said or done in the meeting. If they are to be published, it is often of far more interest to know what was said by the leading speakers than to know what routine business was done, and what resolutions adopted. In such cases the duties of the secretary are arduous, and he should have at least one assistant.

In ordinary society meetings and meetings of boards of managers and trustees, on the contrary, there is no object in reporting the debates; the duty of the clerk, in such cases, is mainly to record what is "done" by the assembly, not what is said by the members. Unless there is a rule to the contrary, he should enter every principal motion [§ 6] that is before the assembly, whether it is adopted or rejected; and where there is a division [see voting, § 38], or where the vote is by ballot, he should enter the number of votes on each side; and when the voting is by yeas and nays [§ 38], he should enter a list of the names of those voting on each side. He should indorse on the reports of committees the date of their reception, and what further action was taken upon them, and preserve them among the records, for which he is responsible.

He should, in the minutes, make a brief summary of a report* that has been agreed to, except where it contains resolutions, in which case the resolutions will be entered in full as adopted by the assembly, and not as if it was the report accepted. The proceedings of the committee of the whole [§ 32], or while acting informally [§ 33], should not be entered on the minutes. Before an adjournment without day, it is customary to read over the minutes for approval, if the next meeting of the board or society will not occur for a long period. Where the regular meetings are not separated by too great a time, the minutes are read at the next meeting, and after correction should be adopted. If after their adoption errors should be detected they should be corrected regardless of the time elapsed and of the number of times the minutes have been previously corrected, and without a motion to reconsider, by a simple vote to amend the minutes.

The minutes, and all other official documents that have come before a deliberative assembly, are in the custody of the secre-

---

* If the report is of great importance the assembly should order it "to be entered on the minutes," in which case the clerk copies it in full upon the record.

tary. But they are open to the inspection
of every member, and the chairman can
even direct that certain ones be turned over
to a committee that needs them for the
proper performance of its duties.

The clerk should, previous to each meeting, for the use of the chairman, make out
an order of business [§ 44], showing in
their exact order what is necessarily to
come before the assembly. He should also
have, at each meeting, a list of all standing
committees, and such select committees as
are in existence at the time. When a committee is appointed, he should hand the
names of the committee, and all papers referred to it, to the chairman of the committee, or some other of its members.

Art. VIII. Miscellaneous.

[§§ 42-45.]

42. **A Session** of an assembly is a meeting* which, though it may last for days, is virtually *one meeting,* as a session of a convention; or even months, as a session of Congress; it terminates by an "adjournment without day." The intermediate

---

* In this Manual the term *meeting* is used to denote an assembling together of the members of a deliberative assembly for any length of time, during which there is no separation of the members by adjournment. An adjournment to meet again at some other time, even the same day, terminates the meeting, but not the session, which latter includes all the adjourned meetings. The next meeting, in this case, would be an "adjourned meeting" of the same session.

A *"meeting"* of an assembly is terminated by a temporary adjournment; a *"session"* of an assembly ends with an adjournment without day, and may consist of many meetings. Sometimes a *recess* is taken for a few minutes, and this does not terminate the "meeting."

In ordinary practice a meeting is closed by moving simply "to adjourn;" the society meet again at the time provided either by their rules or by a resolution of the society. If they do not meet till the time for the next regular meeting, as provided in the by-laws, then the adjournment closed the session, and was in effect an adjournment without day. If, however, they had previously fixed the time for the next meeting, either by a direct vote or by adopting a programme of exercises covering several meetings, or even days, in either case the adjournment is in effect to a certain day, and does not close the session. When an assembly has meetings for several days consecutively, they all constitute one session.

adjournments from day to day, or the recesses taken during the day, do not destroy the continuity of the meeting—they in reality constitute one session. Any meeting which is not an adjournment of another meeting commences a new session. In the case of a permanent society, having regular meetings every week, month, or year, for example, each meeting constitutes a separate session of the society, which session, however, can be prolonged by adjourning to another day.

If a principal motion [§ 6] is indefinitely postponed or rejected at one session, while it cannot be introduced again at the same session [see Renewal of a Motion, § 26], it can be at the next, unless it is prohibited by a rule of the assembly. So, a question that has been laid on the table can be introduced as a new motion at any succeeding session, though it could not be done at the same session. The only way to reach it at the same session is to move to "take it from the table" [§ 19].

No one session of the assembly can interfere with the rights of the assembly at any future session,* unless it is expressly so pro-

* Any one session can adopt a rule or resolution of a permanent nature, and it continues in force until it

vided in their constitution, by-laws, or
rules of order, all of which are so guarded
(by requiring notice of amendments, and at
least a two-thirds vote for their adoption)
that they are not subject to sudden changes,
but may be considered as expressing the
deliberate views of the whole society, rather
than the opinions or wishes of any particular meeting. Thus, if the presiding officer
were ill, it would not be competent for one
session of the assembly to elect a chairman
to hold office longer than that session, as it
cannot control or dictate to the next session
of the assembly.

By going through the prescribed routine
of an election to fill the vacancy, giving
whatever notice is required, it could then
legally elect a chairman to hold office while
the vacancy lasted. So it is improper for an
assembly to postpone anything to a day beyond the next succeeding session, and thus
attempt to prevent the next session from
considering the question. On the other
hand, it is not permitted to move a reconsideration [§ 27] of a vote taken at a pre-

---

is rescinded. But these standing rules [§ 49], as they
are termed, do not interfere with future sessions, because at any moment a majority can suspend or
rescind [§ 25] them, or adopt new ones.

vious session [though the motion to reconsider can be called up, provided it was made at the last meeting of the previous session]. Committees can be appointed to report at a future session.

NOTE ON SESSION.—In Congress, and in fact all legislative bodies, the limits of the sessions are clearly defined; but in ordinary societies having a permanent existence, with regular meetings more or less frequent, there appears to be a great deal of confusion upon the subject. Any society is competent to decide what shall constitute one of its sessions, but, where there is no rule on the subject, the common parliamentary law would make each of its regular or special meetings a separate session, as they are regarded in this Manual.

The disadvantages of a rule making a session include all the meetings of an ordinary society, held during a long time, as one year, are very great. [Examine Indefinitely Postpone, § 24, and Renewal of a Motion, § 26.] If members of any society take advantage of the freedom allowed by considering each regular meeting a separate session, and repeatedly renew obnoxious or unprofitable motions, the society can adopt a rule prohibiting the second introduction of any principal question [§ 6] within, say, three or six months after its rejection, or indefinite postponement, or after the society has refused to consider it. But generally it is better to suppress the motion by refusing to consider it [§ 15].

43. **A Quorum** of an assembly is such
a number as is competent to transact its
business. Unless there is a special rule on
the subject, the quorum of every assembly
is a majority of all the members of the assembly. But whenever a society has a permanent existence it is usual to adopt a much
smaller number, the quorum being often
less than one-twentieth of its members; this
becomes a necessity in most large societies,
where only a small fraction of the members
are ever present at a meeting.*

The chairman should not take the chair
till a quorum is present, except where there
is no hope of there being a quorum, and
then no business can be transacted, except
simply to adjourn. So whenever during the
meeting there is found not to be a quorum
present, the only thing to be done is to ad-

---

* While a quorum is competent to transact any
business, it is usually not expedient to transact important business unless there is a fair attendance at
the meeting, or else previous notice of such action has
been given. Unanimous consent cannot be given when
a quorum is not present.

In the English Parliament, the House of Lords, consisting of about four hundred and fifty members, can
proceed to business if three members are present;
and the House of Commons, with about six hundred
and seventy members, requires only forty members for
a quorum. The U. S. Constitution [Art. I, Sec. 5]
provides that a majority of each House of Congress
shall constitute a quorum to do business.

journ; though, if no question is raised about it, the debate can be continued, but no vote taken, except to adjourn.

In committee of the whole the quorum is the same as in the assembly; in any other committee the majority is a quorum, unless the assembly order otherwise, and it must wait for a quorum before proceeding to business. If the number afterwards should be reduced below a quorum, business is not interrupted, unless a member calls attention to the fact; but no question can be decided except when a quorum is present. Boards of trustees, managers, directors, etc., are on the same footing as committees, in regard to a quorum. Their power is delegated to them as a body, and their quorum, or what number shall be present, in order that they may act as a board, is to be decided by the society that appoints the board or committee. If no quorum is specified, then it consists of a majority.*

---

* Care should be taken in amending the rule providing for a quorum. If the rule is stricken out first, then the quorum instantly becomes a majority of all the members, so that in many societies it would be nearly impracticable to secure a quorum to adopt the new rule. The proper way is to amend by striking out certain words [or the whole rule] and inserting certain other words [or the new rule], which is voted on as one question.

44. Order of Business. It is customary for every society having a permanent existence to adopt an order of business for its meetings. When no rule has been adopted, the following is the order:

(1) Reading the Minutes* of the previous meeting (and their approval).

(2) Reports of Standing Committees.

(3) Reports of Select Committees.

(4) Unfinished Business.

(5) New Business.

Boards of managers, trustees, etc., come under the head of standing committees. If a subject has been made a "special order" [§ 13] for the day, it takes precedence of all business except reading the minutes. The "orders of the day" [§ 13], which include business postponed to this meeting, come in with unfinished business.

If it is desired to transact business out of its order, it is necessary to suspend the rules [§ 18], which can only be done by a two-thirds vote; but, as each resolution or report comes up, a majority can at once lay it on

---

* It is not customary, or necessary, when several meetings are held each day, to have the minutes read more than once a day, usually at the first meeting held.

the table [§ 19], and thus reach any question of which they desire to first dispose.*

45. Amendments of Rules of Order. These rules can be amended at any regular meeting of the assembly, by a two-thirds vote, provided the amendment was submitted in writing at the previous regular meeting. And no amendment to constitutions or by-laws shall be permitted, without at least equal notice and a two-thirds vote.†

---

* It is improper to lay on the table or to postpone a class of questions, like reports of committees, or in fact anything but the question before the assembly [See § 19].

† Constitutions, by-laws, and rules of order should always prohibit their being amended by less than a two-thirds vote, and without previous notice of the amendment being given. The object of this notice is to inform the society that the subject-matter of the amendment will be up for consideration and action at a certain time. It is not to be inferred that notice is required to amend this amendment; if this were the case it would be almost impossible to properly amend by-laws, etc. But this last amendment must be germane to the original amendment; no other amendment is in order or can delay action on the original amendment. In many cases the by-laws provide that an amendment must be read at a certain number of regular meetings before being acted upon; the first reading is by the clerk when it is first proposed, and after the last reading it is up for action; so that if it has to be read at three regular meetings, in a society with regular weekly meetings, action on an amendment would be delayed for only two weeks after it was first proposed.

PART II.

ORGANIZATION AND CONDUCT OF BUSINESS.*

Art. IX. Organization and Meetings.

[§§ 46-49.]

46. An Occasional or Mass Meeting.
(*a*) *Organization.* When a meeting is held, which is not one of an organized society, shortly after the time appointed for the meeting, some member of the assembly steps forward and says: "The meeting will please come to order; I move that Mr. A

---

* The exact words used by the chairman or member are in many cases in quotations. It is not to be inferred that these are the only forms permitted, but that these forms are proper and common. They are inserted for the benefit of those unaccustomed to parliamentary forms, and are sufficiently numerous for ordinary meetings.

If pressed for time, the beginner, after reading this section, should begin at § 54, and read the remainder of this second part.

act as chairman of this meeting." Some
one else says, "I second the motion." The
first member then puts the question to vote,
by saying, "It has been moved and seconded
that Mr. A act as chairman of this meeting;
those in favor of the motion will say *aye;*"
and when the affirmative vote is taken, he
says, "those opposed will say *no.*" If the
majority vote in the affirmative, he says,
"The motion is carried; Mr. A will take the
chair." If the motion is lost, he announces
that fact, and calls for the nomination of
some one else for chairman, and proceeds
with the new nomination as in the first
case.*

When Mr. A takes the chair he says,
"The first business in order is the election
of a secretary." Some one then makes a
motion as just described, or he says, "I
nominate Mr. B," when the chairman puts
the question as before. Sometimes several

---

* Sometimes a member nominates a chairman and
no vote is taken, the assembly signifying their approval by acclamation. The member who calls the
meeting to order, instead of making the motion himself, may act as temporary chairman, and say: "The
meeting will please come to order; will some one
nominate a chairman?" He puts the question to vote
on the nomination as described above. In large assemblies, the member who nominates, with one other
member, frequently conducts the presiding officer to
the chair, and the chairman makes a short speech,
thanking the assembly for the honor conferred on
him.

names are called out, and the chairman, as
he hears them, says, "Mr. B is nominated;
Mr. C is nominated," etc.; he then takes a
vote on the first one he heard, putting the
question thus: "As many as are in favor
of Mr. B acting as secretary of this meeting will say *aye*; those opposed will say
no." If the motion is lost the question is
put on Mr. C, and so on, till some one is
elected. The secretary should take his seat
near the chairman, and keep a record of the
proceedings, as described in § 51.

(*b*) *Adoption of Resolutions.* These
two officers are all that are usually necessary for a meeting; so, when the secretary
is elected, the chairman asks, "What is
the further pleasure of the meeting?" If
the meeting is merely a public assembly
called together to consider some special
subject, it is customary at this stage of
the proceedings for some one to offer a
series of resolutions previously prepared,
or else to move the appointment of a committee to prepare resolutions upon the subject. In the first case he rises and says,
"Mr. Chairman;" the chairman responds,
"Mr. C." Mr. C having thus obtained the
floor, then says, "I move the adoption of
the following resolutions," which he then

reads and hands to the chairman;* some one else says, "I second the motion." The chairman sometimes directs the secretary to read the resolutions again, after which he says, "The question is on the adoption of the resolutions just read," and if no one rises immediately, he adds, "Are you ready for the question?" If no one then rises, he says, "As many as are in favor of the adoption of the resolutions just read will say *aye;*" after the ayes have voted, he says, "As many as are of a contrary opinion will say *"no;"* he then announces the result of the vote as follows: "The motion is carried—the resolutions are adopted," or, "The ayes have it—the resolutions are adopted."

(*c*) *Committee to draft Resolutions.* If it is preferred to appoint a committee to

---

* The practice, in legislative bodies, is to send to the clerk's desk all resolutions, bills, etc., the title of the bill and the name of the member introducing it being indorsed on each. In such bodies, however, there are several clerks and only one chairman. In many assemblies there is but one clerk or secretary, and as he has to keep the minutes there is no reason for his being constantly interrupted to read every resolution offered. In such assemblies, unless there is a rule or established custom to the contrary, it is allowable and frequently much better, to hand all resolutions, reports, etc., directly to the chairman. If they were read by the member introducing them, and no one calls for another reading, the chairman can omit reading them when he thinks they are fully understood. For the manner of reading and stating the question, when the resolution contains several paragraphs, see § 44.

draft resolutions, a member, after he has addressed the chair and been recognized, says: "I move that a committee be appointed to draft resolutions expressive of the sense of this meeting on," etc., adding the subject for which the meeting was called. This motion being seconded, the chairman states the question [§ 65] and asks: "Are you ready for the question?" If no one rises he puts the question, and announces the result; and if it is carried, he asks: "Of how many shall the committee consist?" If only one number is suggested, he announces that the committee will consist of that number; if several numbers are suggested, he states the different ones, and then takes a vote on each, beginning with the largest, until one number is selected.

He then inquires: "How shall the committee be appointed?" This is usually decided without the formality of a vote. The committee may be "appointed" by the chair, in which case the chairman names the committee, and no vote is taken; or the committee may be "nominated" by the chair, or the members of the assembly (no member naming more than one, except by unanimous consent), and then the assembly vote on their appointment. When the chairman nominates, after stating the names he puts one question on the entire committee, thus: "As many as are in favor of these gentlemen constituting the committee will say *aye*." If nominations are made by members of the assembly, and more names mentioned than the number of the committee, a separate vote should be taken on each name. (In a mass meeting it is safer to have all committees appointed by the chairman.)

When the committee are appointed they should at once retire and agree upon a report, which should be written out as described in § 53. During their absence other business may be attended to, or the time may be occupied with hearing addresses. Upon their return* the chairman of the committee (who is the one first named on the committee, and who quite commonly, though not necessarily, is the one who made the motion to appoint the committee), avails himself of the first opportunity to obtain the floor [see § 2], when he says: "The

---

* If the chairman sees the committee return to the room, he should, as soon as the member speaking closes, announce that the assembly will now hear the report of the committee on resolutions; or before this announcement he may ask if the committee is prepared to report.

committee appointed to draft resolutions are prepared to report." The chairman tells him that the assembly will now hear the report, which is then read by the chairman of the committee and handed to the presiding officer, upon which the committee is dissolved without any action of the assembly.

A member then moves the "adoption" or "acceptance" of the report, or that "the resolutions be agreed to," which motions have the same effect if carried, namely, to make the resolutions the resolutions of the assembly, just as if the committee had had nothing to do with them.* When one of these motions is made the chairman acts as stated above, when the resolutions were offered by a member. If it is not desired immediately to adopt the resolutions, they can be debated, modified, their consideration postponed, etc., as explained in §§ 55-63.

When through with the business for which the assembly was convened, or when from any other cause it is desirable to close the meeting, some one moves "to adjourn;" if the motion is carried, and no other time for meeting has been appointed, the chairman says: "The motion is carried; this

---

* See note to § 30 for some common errors in acting upon reports.

assembly stands adjourned without day."
[Another method by which the meeting
may be conducted is shown in § 48.]

(*d*) *Additional Officers.* If more officers
are required than a chairman and secretary,
they can be appointed before introducing
the resolutions in the manner described for
those officers; or, the assembly can first
form a temporary organization in the manner already described, only adding "pro
tem." to the title of the officers, thus,
"chairman pro tem."   In this latter case,
as soon as the secretary pro tem. is elected,
a committee is appointed to nominate the
permanent officers, as in the case of a convention [§ 47]. Frequently the presiding
officer is called the President, and sometimes there is a large number of Vice-Presidents appointed for mere complimentary
purposes. The Vice-Presidents in large formal meetings sit on the platform beside the
President, and in his absence, or when he
vacates the chair, the first on the list that
is present should take the chair.

**47. Meeting of a Convention or As-
sembly of Delegates.** If the members of
the assembly have been elected or appointed
as members, it becomes necessary to know

who are properly members of the assembly and entitled to vote, before the permanent organization is effected.   In this case a temporary organization* is made, as already described, by the election of a chairman and secretary "pro-tem.," when the chairman announces, "The next business in order is the appointment of a committee on credentials."   A motion may then be made covering the entire case, thus: "I move that a committee of three on the credentials of members be appointed by the chair, and that the committee report as soon as practicable;" or they may include only one of these details, thus: "I move that a committee be appointed on the credentials of members." In either case the chair proceeds as already described in the cases of committees on resolutions [§ 46 (c)].

On the motion to accept the report of the committee, none can vote except those reported by the committee as having proper credentials.   The committee, beside reporting a list of members with proper credentials, may report doubtful or contested cases, with recommendations, which the assembly may adopt, or reject, or postpone,

---

* Care should be taken to put no one into office, or on a committee, whose right to a seat is doubted.

etc. Only members whose right to their
seats is undisputed can vote.

The chairman, after the question of credentials is disposed of, at least for the time,
announces that "The next business in order is the election of permanent officers of
the assembly." Some one then moves the
appointment of a committee to nominate
the officers, in a form similar to this: "I
move that a committee of three be appointed by the chair to nominate permanent officers of this convention." This motion is
treated as already explained. When the
committee makes its report, some one
moves "that the report of the committee be
accepted, and that the officers nominated
be declared the officers of this convention."*
This motion being carried, the chairman
declares the officers elected, and instantly
calls the new presiding officer to the
chair, and the temporary secretary is at the

---

* Where there is any competition for the offices, it
is better that they be elected by ballot. In this case,
when the nominating committee report, a motion can
be made as follows: "I move that the convention now
proceed to ballot for its permanent officers;" or, "I
move that we now proceed to the election, by ballot,
of the permanent officers of this convention." [See
§ 38 for balloting and other methods of voting.] The
constitutions of permanent societies usually provide
that the officers shall be elected by ballot.

same time replaced. The convention is now organized for work.

48. A Permanent Society. (*a*) *First Meeting.* When it is desired to form a permanent society, those interested in it should see that only the proper persons are invited to be present at a certain time and place. It is not usual in mass meetings or meetings called to organize a society, to commence until ten or fifteen minutes after the appointed time, when some one steps forward and says: "The meeting will please come to order; I move that Mr. A act as chairman of this meeting." Some one "seconds the motion," when the one who made the motion puts it to vote (or, as it is called, "puts the question"), as already described under an "occasional meeting" [§ 46 (*a*)]; and, as in that case, when the chairman is elected he announces as the first business in order, the election of a secretary.

After the secretary is elected, the chairman calls on some member who is most interested in getting up the society to state the object of the meeting. When this member rises he says: "Mr. Chairman." The chairman then announces his name, when the member proceeds to state the object of the meeting. Having finished his remarks, the chairman may call on other members to give their opinions upon the subject, and sometimes a particular speaker is called out by members who wish to hear him. The chairman should observe the wishes of the assembly, and, while being careful not to be too strict, he must not permit any one to occupy too much time and weary the meeting.

When a sufficient time has been spent in this informal way, some one should offer a resolution, so that definite action can be taken. Those interested in getting up the meeting, if it is to be a large one, should have previously agreed upon what is to be done, and be prepared, at the proper time, to offer a suitable resolution, which may be in form similar to this: "Resolved, That it is the sense of this meeting that a society for [state the object of the society] should now be formed in this city." This resolution, when seconded and stated by the chairman, would be open to debate, and be treated as already described [§ 46 (b)]. This preliminary motion could have been offered at the commencement of the meeting, and, if the meeting is a very large one, this would generally be better than to have the informal discussion.

After this preliminary motion has been voted on, or even without waiting for such motion, one like this can be offered: "I move that a committee of five be appointed by the chair to draft a constitution and by-laws for a society for [here state the object], and that they report at an adjourned meeting of this assembly. This motion can be amended [§ 56] by striking out and adding words, etc., and it is debatable.

When this committee is appointed, the chairman may inquire: "Is there any other business to be attended to?" or, "What is the further pleasure of the meeting?" When all business is finished, a motion can be made to adjourn, to meet at a certain place and time, which, when seconded and stated by the chair, is open to debate and amendment. It is usually better to fix the time of the next meeting [see § 63] at an earlier stage of the meeting; and then, when it is desired to close the meeting, move simply "to adjourn," which cannot be amended or debated. When this motion is carried, the chairman says: "This meeting stands adjourned, to meet at," etc., specifying the time and place of the next meeting.

(*b*) *Second Meeting.** At the next meeting the officers of the previous meeting, if
present, serve until the permanent officers
are elected. When the hour arrives for the
meeting, the chairman standing, says,
"The meeting will please come to order;"
as soon as the assembly is seated, he adds,
"The secretary will read the minutes of the
last meeting." If any one notices an error
in the minutes, he can state the fact as
soon as the secretary finishes reading them;
if there is no objection, without waiting for
a motion, the chairman directs the secretary to make the correction. The chairman
then says, "If there is no objection the

---

* Ordinary meetings of a society are conducted like
this second meeting, the chairman, however, announcing the business in the order prescribed by the rules
of the society [§ 44]. For example, after the minutes
are read and approved, he would say, "The next business in order is hearing the reports from the standing committees." He may then call upon each committee in their order for a report. thus: "Has the
committee on applications for membership any report
to make?" In which case the committee may report,
as shown above, or some member of it reply that they
have no report to make. Or. when the chairman
knows that there are but few if any reports to make,
it is better, after making the announcement of the
business, for him to ask, "Have these committees any
reports to make?" After a short pause, if no one
rises to report. he states. "There being no reports
from the standing committees. the next business in
order is hearing the reports of select committees."
when he will act the same as in the case of the standing committees. The chairman should always have a
list of the committees, to enable him to call upon
them, as well as to guide him in the appointment of
new committees.

minutes will stand approved as read" [or "corrected," if any corrections have been made].

He announces as the next business in order, "the hearing of the report of the committee on the Constitution and By-Laws," The chairman of the committee, after addressing "Mr. Chairman" and being recognized, reads the committee's report and then hands it to the chairman.* If no motion is made, the chairman says, "You have heard the report read—what order shall be taken upon it?" Or simply inquires, "What shall be done with the report?" Some one moves its adoption, or still better, moves "the adoption of the constitution reported by the committee, and when seconded, the chairman says, "The question is on the adoption of the constitution reported by the committee." He then reads the first article of the constitution, and asks, "Are there any amendments proposed to this article?" If none are offered, after a pause, he reads the next article, and asks the same question, and proceeds thus until he reads the last article, when he says,

* In large and formal bodies the chairman, before inquiring what is to be done with the report, usually directs the secretary to read it again. See note to § 30 for a few common errors in acting upon reports of committees. [See also note to § 46 (b).]

"The whole constitution having been read, it is open to amendment." Now any one can move amendments to any part of the constitution.

When the chairman thinks it has been modified to suit the wishes of the assembly, he inquires: "Are you ready for the question?" If no one wishes to speak, he puts the question: "As many as are in favor of adopting the constitution as amended will say *aye*;" and then, "As many as are opposed will say *no*." He distinctly announces the result of the vote, which should always be done. If the articles of the constitution are subdivided into sections or paragraphs, then the amendments should be made by sections or paragraphs, instead of by articles.

The chairman now states that the constitution having been adopted, it will be necessary for those wishing to become members to sign it (and pay the initiation fee, if required by the constitution), and suggests, if the assembly is a large one, that a recess be taken for the purpose. A motion is then made to take a recess for say ten minutes, or until the constitution is signed. The constitution being signed, no one is permitted to vote excepting those who have signed it.

The recess having expired, the chairman calls the meeting to order, and says: "The next business in order is the adoption of by-laws." Some one moves the adoption of the by-laws reported by the committee, and they are treated just like the constitution. The chairman then asks: "What is the further pleasure of the meeting?" or states that the next business in order is the election of the permanent officers of the society. In either case some one moves the appointment of a committee to nominate the permanent officers of the society, which motion is treated as already described in § 47. As each officer is elected he replaces the temporary one, and when they are all elected the organization is completed.

If the society is one that expects to own real estate, it should be incorporated according to the laws of the State in which it is situated, and for this purpose some one on the committee on the constitution should consult a lawyer before this second meeting, so that the constitution may conform to the laws. In this case the trustees are usually instructed to take the proper measures to have the society incorporated.

49. **Constitutions, By-Laws, Rules of Order, and Standing Rules.** In forming

a constitution and by-laws it is always best
to procure copies of those adopted by several similar societies, and for the committee, after comparing them, to select one as
the basis of their own, amending each article just as their own report is amended by
the society. When they have completed
amending the constitution it is adopted by
the committee. The by-laws are treated in
the same way; and then, having finished
the work assigned them, some one moves
"that the committee rise, and that the chairman (or some other member) report the
constitution and by-laws to the assembly."
If this is adopted, the constitution and by-
laws are written out, and a brief report
made of this form: "Your committee, appointed to draft a constitution and by-laws,
would respectfully submit the following,
with the recommendation that they be
adopted as the constitution and by-laws of
this society," which is signed by all the
members of the committee that concur in
it. Sometimes the report is only signed by
the chairman of the committee.

In the organization just given it is as-
sumed that both a constitution and by-laws
are adopted. This is not always done;
some societies adopt only a constitution,

and others only by-laws. When both are adopted, the *Constitution* usually contains only the following:

(1) Name and object of the society.
(2) Qualification of members.
(3) Officers, their election and duties.
(4) Meetings of the society (only including what is essential, leaving details to the by-laws).
(5) How to amend the constitution.

These can be arranged in five articles, each article being subdivided into sections. The constitution containing nothing but what is fundamental, it should be made very difficult to amend; usually, previous notice of the amendment is required, and also a two-thirds or three-fourths vote for its adoption [§ 45]. It is better not to require a larger vote than two-thirds; and, where the meetings are frequent, an amendment should not be allowed to be made except at a quarterly or annual meeting, after having been proposed at the previous quarterly meeting.

The *By-Laws* contain all the other standing rules of the society, of such importance that they should be placed out of the power of any one meeting to modify; or they may omit the rules relating to the conduct of business in the meetings, which would then

constitute the *Rules of Order* of the society.
Every society, in its by-laws or rules of order, should adopt a rule like this: "The
rules contained in [specifying the work on
parliamentary practice] shall govern the
society in all cases to which they are applicable, and in which they are not inconsistent with the rules of order (or by-laws)
of this society." Without such a rule, any
one so disposed could cause great trouble
in a meeting.

In addition to the constitution, by-laws,
and rules of order, in nearly every society
resolutions of a permanent nature are oc-
casionally adopted, which are binding on
the society until they are rescinded or modified. These are called *Standing Rules,* and
can be adopted by a majority vote at any
meeting. After they have been adopted,
they cannot be modified at the same session
except by a reconsideration [§ 60]. At
any future session they can be suspended,
modified, or rescinded by a majority vote.
The standing rules, then, comprise those
rules of a society which have been adopted
like ordinary resolutions, without the
previous notice, etc., required for by-laws,
and, consequently future sessions of the
society are at liberty to terminate them

whenever they please. No standing rule
(or other resolution) can be adopted which
conflicts with the constitution, by-laws, or
rules of order.*

Art. X.   Officers and Committees.

50. Chairman or President. It is the
duty of the chairman to call the meeting to
order at the appointed time, to preside at all
the meetings, to announce the business before the assembly in its proper order, to
state and put all questions properly brought
before the assembly, to preserve order and

---

* In practice these various classes of rules are frequently very much mixed. The standing rules of
some societies are really by-laws, as the society cannot suspend them, nor can they be amended until
previous notice is given. This produces confusion
without any corresponding benefit.

Standing Rules should contain only such rules as
are subject to the will of the majority of any meeting, and which it may be expedient to change at any
time, without the delay incident to giving previous
notice. *Rules of Order* should contain only the rules
relating to the orderly transaction of the business in
the meetings of the society. The *By-Laws* should contain all the other rules of the society which are of
too great importance to be changed without giving
notice to the society of such change; provided that
the most important of these can be placed in a *Constitution* instead of in the by-laws. These latter three
should provide for their amendment. The rules of
order should provide for their suspension. The by-
laws sometimes provide for the suspension of certain
articles [see note to § 18.]

decorum, and to decide all questions of order (subject to an appeal). When he "puts a question" to vote, and when speaking upon an appeal, he should stand;* in all other cases he can sit. In all cases where his vote would affect the result, or where the vote is by ballot, he can vote. When a member rises to speak, he should say, "Mr. Chairman," and the chairman should reply, "Mr. A;" he should not interrupt a speaker so long as he is in order, but should listen to his speech, which should be addressed to him and not to the assembly. The chairman should be careful to abstain from the appearance of partisanship, but he has the right to call another member to the chair while he addresses the assembly on a question; when speaking to a question or order he does not leave the chair.

HINTS TO INEXPERIENCED CHAIRMEN.—While in the chair, have beside you your Constitution, By-Laws and Rules of Order, which should be studied until you are perfectly familiar with them. You cannot tell the moment you may need this knowledge. If a member asks what motion to make in order to attain a certain object, you should be able to tell him at once. [See § 55.]

---

* In meetings of boards of managers, committees, and other small bodies, the chairman usually retains his seat, and even members in speaking do not rise.

You should memorize the list of ordinary motions arranged in their order of precedence [see page 10], and should be able to refer to the Table of Rules so quickly that there would be no delay in deciding all points contained in it.

You should know all the business to come regularly before the meeting, and call for it in its regular order. Have with you a list of members of all committees, to guide you in nominating new committees.

As soon as a motion is made and seconded, distinctly announce what question is before the assembly; so, when a vote is taken, announce the result and also what question, if any, is then pending. [See § 54 for the proper forms.] Never wait for mere routine motions to be seconded, when you know no one objects to them. [See § 65.]

If a member ignorantly makes an improper motion, politely suggest the proper one. If it is moved "to lay the question on the table until a certain time," as the motion is improper, ask if the intention is "to postpone the question to that time"; if the answer is yes, then state that the question is on the postponement to that time. If it is moved simply "to postpone the question" without stating a time, do not rule it out of order, but ask the mover if he wishes "to postpone the question indefinitely" (which kills it), or "to lay it on the table" (which enables it to be taken up at any other time); then state the question in accordance with the motion he intended to make. So if, after a report has been presented and read, a member moves that "it be received," ask him if he means to move "its adoption" [or "acceptance," which is the same thing], as the report has been already received. [No vote should be taken on receiving a report, which merely brings it before the assembly and allows it to be read, unless someone objects to its reception. See note § 30.]

The chairman of a committee usually has the most to say in reference to questions before the committee; but the chairman of an ordinary deliberative assembly. especially a large one, should, of all the members, have the least to say upon the merits of pending questions.

Never interrupt members while speaking, simply because you know more about the matter than they do; never get excited; never be unjust to the most troublesome member, nor take advantage of his ignorance of parliamentary law, even though a temporary good is accomplished thereby.

Know all about parliamentary law, but do not try to show off your knowledge. Never be technical, nor be any more strict than is absolutely necessary for the good of the meeting. Use your judgment; the assembly may be of such a nature through its ignorance of parliamentary usages and peaceable disposition, that a strict enforcement of the rules, instead of assisting, would greatly hinder business: but in large assemblies, where there is much work to be done, and especially where there is liability to trouble, the only safe course is to require a strict observance of the rules.

51. The Clerk, Secretary, or Recording Secretary, as he is variously called, should keep a record of the proceedings, the character of which depends upon the kind of meeting. In an occasional or mass meeting, the record usually amounts to nothing, but he should always record every resolution or motion that is adopted.

In a convention it is often desirable to keep a full record for publication, and where it lasts for several days, it is usual, and generally best, to appoint one or more assitant clerks. Frequently it is a tax on the judgment of the clerk to decide what to enter on the record, or the "Minutes," as it is usually called. Sometimes the points of each speech should be entered, and at other times only the remark that the question was discussed by Messrs. A, B, and C in the affirmative, and Messrs. D, E, and F in the negative. Every resolution that is adopted should be entered, which can be done in this form: "On motion of . Mr. D it was resolved that, etc."

Sometimes a convention does its work by having certain topics previously assigned to certain speakers, who deliver formal addresses or essays, the subjects of which are afterwards open for discussion in short speeches—of five minutes, for instance. In such cases the minutes are very brief, unless they are to be published, when they should contain either the entire addresses, or carefully prepared abstracts of them, and should show the drift of the discussion that followed each one. In permanent societies, where the minutes are not published, they consist of a record of what was done and not what was said, and should be kept in a book. The secretary should never make in the minutes any criticism, either favorable or otherwise, upon anything said or done in a meeting.

The *Form* of the *Minutes* can be as follows:

At a regular meeting of the M. L. Society, held in their hall, on Thursday evening, March 16, 1875, Mr. A in the chair, and Mr. B acting as secretary, the minutes of the previous meeting were read and approved. The committee on Applications reported the names of Messrs. C and D as applicants for membership, and on motion of Mr. F they were admitted as members. The committee on ——— reported through Mr. G a series of resolutions, which were thoroughly discussed and amended, and finally adopted, as follows:
    Resolved, That   *   *   *   *   *
*   *   *   *   *   *   *   *
On motion of Mr. L the society adjourned.
                              L——— B———,
                                      Secretary.

If the proceedings are to be published, the secretary should always examine the published proceedings of similar meetings, so as to conform to the custom, excepting where it is manifestly improper.

The constitution, by-laws, rules of order, and standing rules should all be written in one book, leaving every other page blank; and whenever an amendment is made to any of them, it should be immediately entered on the page opposite to the article amended, with a reference to the date and page of the minutes where is recorded the action of the society.

The secretary has the custody of all papers belonging to the society, not especially under charge of any other officer. Sometimes his duties are also of a financial kind, when he should make such reports as are prescribed in the next section.

52. Treasurer. The duties of this officer vary in different societies. In probably the majority of cases he acts as a banker, merely holding the funds deposited with him, and paying them out on the order of the society signed by the secretary. His annual report, which is always required, in this case consists of merely a statement of the amount on hand at the commencement of the year, the amount received during the year (stating from what sources received), the total amount paid out by order of the society, and the balance on hand. When this report is presented it is referred to an "auditing committee," consisting of one or two persons, who examine the treasurer's books and vouchers, and certify on his report that they "have examined his accounts and vouchers and find them correct, and the balance on hand is," etc., stating the amount on hand. The auditing committee's report being accepted is equivalent to a resolution of the society to the same effect, namely, that the treasurer's report is correct.

In the case here supposed the real financial statement is made either by the board of trustees, or by the secretary or some other officer, according to the constitution of the society. The principles involved are, that every officer who receives money is to account for it in a report to the society, and that whatever officer is responsible for the disbursements shall report them to the society. If the secretary, as in many societies, is really responsible for the expenses, the treasurer merely paying upon his order, then the secretary should make a full report of these expenses, so classified as to enable the society to readily see the amounts expended for various purposes.

It should always be remembered that the financial report is made for the information of members. The details of dates and separate payments for the same object are a hindrance to its being understood, and are useless, as it is the duty of the auditing committee to examine into the details and see if the report is correct.

Every disbursing officer should be careful to get a receipt whenever he makes a payment; these receipts should be preserved in regular order, as they are the vouchers for the payments, which must be examined by the auditing committee. Disbursing officers cannot be too careful in keeping their accounts, and they should insist upon having their accounts audited every time they make a report, as by this means any error is quickly detected and may be corrected. When the society has accepted the auditing committee's report that the financial report is correct, the disbursing officer is relieved from the responsibility of the past, and if his vouchers were lost afterwards it would cause no trouble. The best form for these financial reports depends upon the kind of society, and is best determined by examining those made in similar societies.

The following form can be varied to suit most cases [when the statement of receipts and expenses is very long, it is often desirable to specify the amounts received from one or two particular sources, which can be done immediately after stating the total receipts; the same course can be taken in regard to the expenditures] :

Treasurer's Report.

The undersigned, Treasurer of the M. L. Society, begs leave to submit the following annual report:

The balance on hand at the commencement of the year was ——— dollars and ——— cents. There was received from all sources during the year ——— dollars and ——— cents; during the same time the expenses amounted to ——— dollars and ——— cents, leaving a balance on hand of ——— dollars and ——— cents.

The annexed statement of receipts and expenditures will show in detail the sources from which the receipts were obtained, and the objects to which the expenditures have been applied.

All of which is respectfully submitted.

S——— M———,
Treasurer M. L. S.

The "statement of receipts and expenditures" can be made by simply giving a list of receipts, followed by a list of expenses, and finishing up with the balance on hand. The auditing committee's certificate to the correctness of the account should be written on the statement. Often the statement is made out in the form of an account, as follows:

Dr. The M. L. S. in acct. with S. M., Treas. *Cr.*

1875.			1875.		
Dec. 31.	To rent of hall - -	$500.00	Jan. 1.	By bal. on hand from	
	" gas - - - - -	80.00		last year's account	$ 21.13
	" stationery - - -	26.50	Dec. 31.	By initiation fees - -	95.00
	" janitor - - - -	360.00		" members dues -	860.00
	" balance on hand	24.63		" fines - - - - -	15.00
		$991.13			$991.13

We do hereby certify that we have examined the accounts and vouchers of the treasurer, and find them correct; and that the balance in his hands is twenty-four dollars and sixty-three cents.

R. V.,
J. L., } *Audit Com.*

53. Committees. In small assemblies, especially in those where but little business is done, there is not much need of committees. But in large assemblies, or in those doing a great deal of business, committees are of the utmost importance. When a committee is properly selected, in nine cases out of ten its action decides that of the assembly. A committee for *action* should be small, and consist only of those heartily in favor of the proposed action. A committee for deliberation or investigation, on the contrary, should be larger, and represent all parties in the assembly, so that its opinion will carry with it as great weight as possible. The usefulness of the committee will be greatly impaired if any important faction of the assembly be unrepresented on the committee. The appointment of a committee is fully explained in § 46 (*c*).

The first member named on a committee is its chairman, and it is his duty to call together the committee and preside at its meetings, unless the committee by a majority of its number elects another chairman, which it is competent to do, unless the assembly has appointed the chairman. If he is absent, or from any cause fails or declines to call a meeting, it is the duty of the committee to assemble on the call of any two of its members. The committee is a miniature assembly, being able to act only when a quorum is present. If a paper is referred to them, they must not deface it in any way, but write their amendments on a separate sheet. If they originate the paper, all amendments must be incorporated in it. When they originate the paper, usually one member has previously prepared a draft, which is read entirely through, and then read by paragraphs, the chairman pausing after each paragraph, and asking: "Are there any amendments proposed to this paragraph?" No vote is taken on the adoption of the separate paragraphs; but, after the whole paper has been read in this

way, it is open to amendment generally by
striking out any paragraph or inserting
new ones, or by substituting an entirely new
paper for it.   When it has been amended to
suit the committee, they should adopt it as
their report, and direct the chairman or
some other member to report it to the assembly.   It is then written out, usually commencing in a style similar to this: "The
committee to which was referred [state the
matter referred], beg leave to submit the
following report;" or, "Your committee appointed to [specify the object], would
respectfully report," etc.   It usually closes
thus: "All of which is respectfully submitted," followed by the signatures of all
the members concurring in the report, or
sometimes by only that of the chairman.

If the minority submit a report, it commences thus: "The undersigned, a minority
of the committee appointed," etc., continuing as the regular report of the committee.
After the committee's report has been read
it is usual to allow the minority to present
their report; but it cannot be acted upon
except by a motion to substitute it for the
report of the committee.   When the committee's report is read they are discharged
without any motion.   A motion to refer the

paper back to the same committee (or to recommit), if adopted, revives the committee.

Art. XI. Introduction of Business.

54. Any member wishing to bring business before the assembly should, unless it is very simple, write down, in the form of a motion, what he would like to have the assembly adopt, thus:

Resolved, That the thanks of this convention be tendered to the citizens of this community for their hearty welcome and generous hospitality.

When there is no other business before the assembly, he rises and addresses the chairman by his title, thus: "Mr. Chairman," who immediately recognizes him by announcing his name.* He then, having the floor, says, "I move the adoption of the following resolution," which he reads and

---

* If the chairman has any special title (as President, for instance), he should be addressed by it, thus: "Mr. President." Sometimes the chairman recognizes the speaker by merely bowing to him, but the proper course is to announce his name.

hands to the chairman.* Some one else seconds the motion, and the chairman says, "It has been moved and seconded that the following resolution be adopted," when he reads the resolution; or he may read the resolution and then state the question thus: "The question is on the adoption of the resolution just read." The merits of the resolution are then open to discussion, but before any member can discuss the question or make any motion, he must first obtain the floor as just described. After the chairman states the question, if no one rises to speak, or when he thinks the debate closed, he asks, "Are you ready for the question?"† If no one then rises, he puts the question in a form similar to the following: "The question is on the adoption of the resolution which you have heard read; as many as are in favor of its adoption will say *aye*." When the ayes have voted, he says, "As many as are of a contrary opinion will say *no*." He then announces the result, stating that the motion is carried, or lost, as the case may

---

* Or, when he is recognized by the chair, he may say that he wishes to offer the following resolutions, which he reads and then moves their adoption. In very large bodies the name of the mover should be indorsed on the written resolutions, especially if much business is to be transacted.

† See second note to § 65.

be, in the following form: "The motion is carried—the resolution is adopted;" or, "The ayes have it,—the resolution is adopted." A majority of the votes cast is sufficient for the adoption of any motion, excepting those mentioned in § 39. [For other forms of stating and putting questions see § 65. For other illustrations of the common practice in introducing business, and in making various motions see §§ 46-48.]

Art. XII. Motions.

55. Motions Classified According to their Object. Instead of immediately adopting or rejecting a resolution as originally submitted, it may be desirable to dispose of it in some other way, and for this purpose various motions have come into use, which can be made while a resolution is being considered, and, for the time being, supersede it. No one can make any of these motions while another member has the floor, excepting as shown in the Table of Rules: the circumstances under which each motion can be made are shown in the Order of Precedence of Motions, p. 10.

When a motion has been recognized by

the chair as pending it must, if not withdrawn, be disposed of by a vote unless the
meeting adjourn while it is pending.   It
may be interrupted by motions having precedence of it, but as soon as they are acted
on, if this action does not dispose of the
original question, then the consideration of
that question is resumed without any new
motion being made.

The following list comprises most of
these motions, arranged in eight classes, according to the object for which each motion is used:

MOTIONS CLASSIFIED ACCORDING TO
THEIR OBJECT.

[The object to be attained is printed thus: "(2)
To defer action;" the motions to accomplish this
object are printed in *Italics* under the object, and
marked (*a*), (*b*), etc.; the difference in the use of
these motions is shown in the section referred to.]

(1) To Modify or Amend................[§ 56]

    (*a*) *Amend.*
    (*b*) *Commit or Refer.*

(2) To Defer Action....................[§ 57]
    (*a*) *Postpone to a Certain Time.*
    (*b*) *Lay on the Table.*

(3) To Suppress Debate.................[§ 58]
    (*a*) *Previous Question.*
    (*b*) *An Order Limiting or Closing Debate.*

(4) To Suppress the Question............[§ 59]
    (*a*) *Objection to its Consideration.*
    (*b*) *Postpone Indefinitely.*
    (*c*) *Lay on the Table.*

(5) To Consider a Question the Second
      Time ....[§ 60]
      (a) *Reconsider.*
(6) Order and Rules....................[§ 61]
      (a) *Orders of the Day.*
      (b) *Special Orders.*
      (c) *Suspension of the Rules.*
      (d) *Questions of Order.*
      (e) *Appeal.*
(7) Miscellaneous ....[§ 62]
      (a) *Reading of Papers.*
      (b) *Withdrawal of a Motion.*
      (c) *Questions of Privilege.*
(8) To Close a Meeting.................[§ 63]
      (a) *Fix the Time to which to Adjourn.*
      (b) *Adjourn.*

56. To Modify or Amend. (*a*) *Amend.*
If it is desired to modify the question in any
way, the proper motion to make is "to
amend," either by "adding" words, or by
"striking out" words; or by "striking out
certain words and inserting others;" or by
"substituting" a different motion on the
same subject for the one before the assembly; or by "dividing the question" into two
or more questions, as the mover specifies,
so as to get a separate vote on any particular point or points. Sometimes the enemies
of a measure seek to amend it in such a
way as to divide its friends, and thus defeat it.

When the amendment has been moved
and seconded, the chairman should always

state the question distinctly, so that every
one may know exactly what is before them,
reading first the paragraph which it is proposed to amend; then the words to be struck
out, if there are any; next, the words to be
inserted, if any; and finally, the paragraph
as it will stand if the amendment is adopted.
He then states that the question is on the
adoption of the amendment, which is open
to debate, the remarks being confined to
the merits of the amendment, only going
into the main question so far as is necessary
in order to ascertain the propriety of adopting the amendment.

This amendment can be amended, but an
"amendment of an amendment" cannot be
amended.   None of the undebatable motions mentioned in § 35, except to fix the
time to which to adjourn, to extend the
limits of debate, and to close or limit debate, can be amended, nor can the motion
to postpone indefinitely.

(b) *Commit or Refer*.   If the original
question is not well digested, or needs more
amendment than can well be made in the
assembly, it is usual to move "to refer it to
a committee."   This motion can be made
while an amendment is pending, and it
opens the whole merits of the question to

debate. This motion can be amended by specifying the number of the committee, or how they shall be appointed, or when they shall report, or by giving them any other instructions. [See § 53 on committees, and § 46 (*c*) on their appointment.]

57. To Defer Action. (*a*) *Postpone to a Certain Time.* If it is desired to defer action upon a question till a particular time, the proper motion to make is "to postpone it to that time." This motion allows of but limited debate, which must be confined to the propriety of the postponement to that time; it can be amended by altering the time, and this amendment allows of the same debate. The time specified must not be beyond that session [§ 42] of the assembly, except it be the next session, in which case it comes up with the unfinished business at the next session. This motion can be made when a motion to amend, or to commit, or to postpone indefinitely, is pending.

(*b*) *Lay on the Table.* Instead of postponing a question to a particular time, it may be desired to lay it aside temporarily until some other question is disposed of, retaining the privilege of resuming its con-

sideration at any time.* The only way to
accomplish this is to move that the question
"lie on the table." This motion allowing of
neither debate nor amendment, the chairman immediately puts the question; if carried, the whole matter is laid aside till the
assembly vote to "take it from the table"
(which latter motion is undebatable and
possesses no privilege). Sometimes this
motion is used to suppress a measure, as
shown in § 59 (c).

58. To Suppress Debate.†   (a) *Previous Question.* While, as a general rule,
free debate is allowed upon every motion,‡
which, if adopted, has the effect of adopt-

---

* In Congress this motion is commonly used to
defeat a measure, though it does not prevent a majority from taking it up at any other time. Some
societies prohibit a question from being taken up from
the table, except by a two-thirds vote. This rule de-
prives the society of the advantages of the motion
"to lay on the table," because it would not be safe to
lay a question aside temporarily, if one-third of the
assembly were opposed to the measure, as that one-
third could prevent it ever being taken from the table.
A bare majority should not have the power; in ordinary societies, to adopt or reject a question, or prevent its consideration, without debate. [See note at
end of § 35, on the principles involved in making
questions undebatable.]

† These motions are strictly for closing or limiting
debate, and may be used by either the friends or
enemies of a measure. The enemies of a measure may
also close debate by suppressing the question itself,
as shown in § 59 (a, c).

‡ Except an "objection to the consideration of the
question" [§ 59 (a)]. See note to § 35 for a full
discussion of this subject of debate.

ing the original question or removing it from before the assembly for the session, yet, to prevent a minority from making an improper use of this privilege, it is necessary to have methods by which debate can be closed and final action can at once be taken upon a question.

To accomplish this when any debatable question is before the assembly, it is only necessary for some one to obtain the floor and "call for the previous question;" this call being seconded, the chairman, as it allows of no debate, instantly puts the question thus: "Shall the main question be now put?" If this is carried by a two-thirds vote [§ 39] all debate instantly ceases, excepting that in case the pending measure has been reported from a committee the member reporting it is, as in all other cases, entitled to the floor to close the debate; after which the chairman immediately puts the questions to the assembly, first on the motion to commit, if it is pending; if this is carried, of course the subject goes to the committee; if, however, it fails, the vote is next taken on amendments, and finally on the resolution as amended.

If a motion to postpone, either definitely or indefinitely, or a motion to reconsider, or

an appeal is pending, the previous question
is exhausted by the vote on the postponement, reconsideration or appeal, and does
not cut off debate upon any other motions
that may be pending. If the call for the
previous question fails—that is, the debate
is not cut off—the debate continues the
same as if this motion had not been made.
The previous question can be called for
simply on an amendment; and after the
amendment has been acted upon, the main
question is again open to debate.*

(b) *An Order Limiting or Closing Debate.* Sometimes, instead of cutting off debate entirely, by ordering the previous question, it is desirable to allow of but very limited debate. In this case a motion is made
to limit the time allowed each speaker, or
the number of speeches on each side, or to
appoint a time at which debate shall close
and the question be put. The motion may
be made to limit debate on an amendment;
in which case the main question would afterwards be open to debate and amendment;
or it may be made simply on an amendment
of an amendment.

---

* As the Previous Question is so generally misunderstood, it would be well to read also what is said
upon this subject in § 20.

In ordinary societies, where harmony is so important, a two-thirds vote should be required for the adoption of any of the above motions to cut off or limit debate.*

59. To Suppress the Question. (*a*) *Objection to the Consideration of a Question.* Sometimes a resolution is introduced that the assembly do not wish to consider at all, because it is profitless, or irrelevant to the objects of the assembly, or for other reasons. The proper course to pursue in such cases is for some one, as soon as it is introduced, to "object to the consideration of the question." This objection not requiring a second, the chairman immediately puts the question: "Will the assembly consider this question?" If decided in the negative by a two-thirds vote, the question is immediately dismissed, and cannot be again introduced during that session. This objection must be made when the question is first introduced, before it has been debated, and it can be made when another member has the floor.

---

* In the House of Representatives these motions require only a majority vote for their adoption. In the Senate, on the contrary, not even two-thirds of the members can force a measure to its passage without allowing debate, the Senate rules not recognizing the above motions.

(b) *Postpone Indefinitely.* After the question has been debated, the only proper way to suppress it for the session is to vote it down, or to postpone it indefinitely, both of which have the same effect. If the motion to indefinitely postpone is lost, there is still an opportunity for defeating the resolution. It cannot be made while any motion except the original or main question is pending, but it can be made after an amendment has been acted upon, and the main question, as amended, is before the assembly. It opens the merits of the main question to debate to as great an extent as if the main question were before the assembly, and therefore it is necessary also to move the previous question in order to cut off debate and bring the assembly to an immediate vote, just the same as if the question were on the adoption of the resolution.

(c) *Lay on the Table.** If there is no possibility during the remainder of the session of obtaining a majority vote for taking up the question, then the quickest way of suppressing it is to move "to lay the ques-

---

* The use of this motion to suppress a question is common, but, as shown in note at close of § 39, a question should not be suppressed and debate prevented by less than a two-thirds vote. See note at close of § 19.

tion on the table ;" which, allowing of no debate, enables the majority to instantly lay the question on the table, from which it cannot be taken without their consent.

From its high rank [see p. 10] and undebatable character, this motion is very commonly used to suppress a question, but, as shown in § 57 (*b*), its effect is merely to lay the question aside till the assembly choose to consider it, and it only suppresses the question so long as there is a majority opposed to its consideration.

60. To Consider a Question a Second Time. *Reconsider.* When a question has been once adopted, rejected, or suppressed it cannot be again considered during that session [§ 42], except by a motion to "reconsider the vote" on that question. This motion can only be made by one who voted* on the prevailing side, and on the day the vote was taken which it is proposed to reconsider, or on the next succeeding day. It can be made and entered on the minutes in the midst of debate, even when another

---

* In Congress, if the yeas and nays were not taken on the vote, any one can move the reconsideration. The yeas and nays are, however, ordered on all important votes in Congress, which is not the case in ordinary societies.

member has the floor, but cannot be considered until there is no question before the assembly, when, if called up, it takes precedence of every motion except to adjourn and to fix the time to which the assembly shall adjourn.

A motion to reconsider a vote on a debatable question, opens to debate the entire merits of the original motion. If the question to be reconsidered is undebatable, then the reconsideration is undebatable.

If the motion to reconsider is carried, the chairman announces that the question now recurs on the adoption of the question the vote on which has been just reconsidered; the original question is now in exactly the same condition that it was in before the first vote was taken on its adoption, and must be disposed of by vote.

When a motion to reconsider is entered on the minutes, it need not be called up by the mover till the next meeting, on a succeeding day.* If he fails to call it up then, any one else can do so. But should there be

---

* If the assembly has not adopted these or similar rules, this paragraph would not apply; but this motion to reconsider would, like any other motion, fall to the ground if not acted upon before the close of the session at which the original vote was adopted.

no succeeding meeting, either adjourned or regular, within a month, then the effect of the motion to reconsider terminates with the adjournment of the meeting at which it was made, and any one can call it up at that meeting.

In general no motion (except to adjourn) that has been once acted upon can again be considered during the same session, except by a motion to reconsider. [The motion to adjourn can be renewed if there has been progress in business or debate, and it cannot be reconsidered.] But this rule does not prevent the renewal of any of the motions mentioned in § 7, provided the question before the assembly has in any way changed; for in this case, while the motions are nominally the same, they are in fact different.*

61. **Order and Rules.** (a) *Orders of the Day.* Sometimes an assembly decides that certain questions shall be considered at a particular time, and when that time ar-

* Thus to move to postpone a resolution is a different question from moving to postpone it after it has been amended. A motion to suspend the rules for a certain purpose cannot be renewed at the same meeting, but can be at an adjourned meeting. A call for the orders of the day, that has been negatived, cannot be renewed while the question then before the assembly is still under consideration. [See § 27 for many peculiarities of this motion, and § 25 for the motion to Rescind.]

rives those questions constitute what is termed the "orders of the day;" and if any member "calls for the orders of the day," as it requires no second, the chairman immediately puts the question thus: "Will the assembly now proceed to the orders of the day?" If carried, the subject under consideration is laid aside, and the questions appointed for that time are taken up in their order. When the time arrives the chairman may state that fact, and put the above question without waiting for a motion; or, he can announce the orders of the day without taking any vote, if no one objects. If the motion fails, the call for the orders of the day cannot be renewed until the subject then before the assembly is disposed of.*

(b) *Special Order.* If a subject is of such importance that it is desired to consider it at a special time, in preference to the orders of the day and established order of business, then a motion should be made to make the question a "special order" for that particular time. This motion requires a two-thirds vote for its adoption, because it is really a suspension of the rules, and it is in order whenever a motion to suspend

---

* See § 13 for a fuller explanation.

the rules is in order. If a subject is a special order for a particular day, then on that day it supersedes all business except the reading of the minutes. A special order can be postponed by a majority vote. If two special orders are made for the same day, the one first made takes precedence.

(*c*) *Suspension of the Rules.* It is necessary for every assembly, if discussion is allowed, to have rules to prevent its time being wasted, and to enable it to accomplish the object for which the assembly was organized; and yet at times their best interests are subserved by suspending their rules temporarily. In order to do this some one makes a motion "to suspend the rules that interfere with," etc., stating the object of the suspension. If this motion is carried by a two-thirds vote, then the particular thing for which the rules were suspended can be done. By "general consent," that is, if no one objects, the rules relating to the transaction of business can at any time be ignored without the formality of a motion.

(*d*) *Questions of Order.* It is the duty of the chairman to enforce the rules and preserve order, and when any member notices a breach of order he can call for the enforcement of the rules. In such cases, when he rises he usually says: "Mr. Chairman, I rise to a point of order." The chairman then directs the speaker to take his seat, and, having heard the point of order, decides the question and permits the first speaker to resume his speech, directing him to abstain from any conduct that was decided to be out of order. When a speaker has transgressed the rules of decorum he cannot continue his speech if any one objects, unless permission is granted him by a vote of the assembly. Instead of the above method, when a member uses improper language, some one says: "I call the gentleman to order," when the chairman decides as before whether the language is disorderly.

(*e*) *Appeal.* While on all questions of order, and of interpretation of the rules, and of priority of business, it is the duty of the chairman to first decide the question, it is the privilege of any member to "appeal from the decision." If the appeal is seconded, the chairman states his decision, and that it has been appealed from, and then states the question thus: "Shall the decision of the chair stand as the judgment of the assembly [or society, convention, etc.]?"

The chairman can then, without leaving the chair, state the reasons for his decision, after which it is open to debate (no member speaking more than once), excepting in the following cases, when it is undebatable: (1) When it relates to transgressions of the rules of speaking, or to some indecorum, or to the priority of business, and (2) when the previous question was pending at the time the question of order was raised. After the vote is taken, the chairman states that the decision of the chair is sustained, or reversed, as the case may be.

62. Miscellaneous. (*a*) *Reading of Papers* and (*b*) *Withdrawal of a Motion.* If a speaker wishes to read a paper, or a member to withdraw his motion after it has been stated by the chair, it is necessary, if any one objects, to make a motion to grant the permission.

(*c*) *Questions of Privilege.* Should any disturbance occur during the meeting, or anything affecting the rights of the assembly, or any of the members, any member may "rise to a question of privilege," and state the matter, which the chairman decides to be, or not to be, a matter of privilege.* (From the chairman's decision of

---

* A personal explanation is not a matter of privilege. It can be made only by leave of the assembly implied or expressed.

course an appeal can be taken.)   If the question is one of privilege, it supersedes, for the time being, the business before the assembly; its consideration can be postponed to another time, or the previous question can be ordered on it so as to stop debate, or it can be laid on the table, or referred to a committee to examine and report upon it.   As soon as the question of privilege is in some way disposed of, the debate which was interrupted is resumed.

63. To Close the Meeting. (a)   *Fix the Time to which to Adjourn.*

If it is desired to have an adjourned meeting of the assembly, it is best some time before its close to move, "That when this assembly adjourns, it adjourns to meet at such a time," specifying the time. This motion can be amended by altering the time, but if made when another question is before the assembly, neither the motion nor the amendment can be debated. If made when no other business is before the assembly, it stands as any other main question, and can be debated. This motion can be made even while the assembly is voting on the motion to adjourn, but not when another member has the floor.

(b) *Adjourn.*   In order to prevent an

assembly from being kept in session an un-
reasonably long time, it is necessary to have
a rule limiting the time that the floor can
be occupied by any one member at one
time.* When it is desired to close the meeting, unless the member who has the floor
will yield it, the only resource is to wait till
his time expires, and then a member who
gets the floor should move "to adjourn."
The motion being seconded, the chairman
instantly puts the question, as it allows of
no amendment or debate; and if decided in
the affirmative he says, "The motion is carried; this assembly stands adjourned." If
the assembly is one that will have no other
meeting, instead of "adjourned," he says,
"adjourned without day," or *"sine die."* If
previously it had been decided when they
adjourned to adjourn to a particular time,
then he states that the assembly stands adjourned to that time. If the motion to adjourn is qualified by specifying the time,
as, "to adjourn to to-morrow evening," it
cannot be made when any other question is
before the assembly; like any other main
motion, it can then be amended and debated.†

---

* Ten minutes is allowed by these rules.
† See § 11 for effect of an adjournment upon unfinished business.

Art. XIII.   Miscellaneous.

64. Debate. All remarks must be addressed to the chairman and confined to the question before the assembly, avoiding all personalities and reflections upon any one's motives. It is usual for permanent assemblies to adopt rules limiting the number of times any one can speak to the same question, and the time allowed for each speech,* as otherwise one member, while he could speak only once to the same question, might defeat a measure by prolonging his speech, and declining to yield the floor except for a motion to adjourn. In ordinary assemblies two speeches should be allowed each member (except upon an appeal), and these rules also limit the time for each speech to ten minutes. A member can be permitted by a two-thirds vote to speak oftener or longer whenever it is desired, and the motion granting such permission cannot be debated. However, if greater freedom is wanted, it is only necessary to consider the

---

* In Congress, the House of Representatives allows from each member only one speech of one hour's length; the Senate allows two speeches without limit as to length.

question informally, or if the assembly is
large, to go into committee of the whole.*
If, on the other hand, it is desired to limit
the debate more, or close it altogether, it
can be done by a two-thirds vote, as shown
in § 58 (*b*).

**65. Forms of Stating and Putting
Questions.** Whenever a motion has been
made and seconded, it is the duty of the
chairman, if the motion is in order, to state
the question, so that the assembly may
know what question is before them. The
seconding of a motion is required to prevent the introduction of a question when
only one member is in favor of it, and consequently but little attention is paid to it in
mere routine motions, or when it is evident
that many are in favor of the motion; in
such cases the chairman assumes that the
motion is seconded.

Often in routine work the chairman puts
the question without waiting for even a
motion,† as few persons like to make such

* See §§ 32, 33.

† A presiding officer can frequently expedite business
by not waiting for a motion or even taking a vote on
a question of routine. In such a case he announces
that if there is no objection such will be considered
the action of the assembly. For example, when the
treasurer's report is read he can say, "If there is no

formal motions, and much time would be wasted by waiting for them (but the chairman can only do this as long as no one objects). The following motions, however, do not have to be seconded: (*a*) a call for the orders of the day; (*b*) a call to order, or the raising of any question of order; and (*c*) an objection to the consideration of a question.

One of the commonest forms of stating a question is to say that, "It is moved and seconded that," and then give the motion; or, in case of resolutions, it might be stated in this way (after they have been read): "The question is on the adoption of the resolutions just read."

In some cases, in order to state the question clearly, the chairman should do much more than merely repeat the motion, and say that the question is on its adoption. In the case of an appeal, he should state the decision of the chair (and, if he thinks proper, the reasons for it), and that the decision has been appealed from; he then says, "The question is, shall the decision of the chair stand as the judgment of the

---

objection the report will be referred to an auditing committee, consisting of Messrs. A. and B,"—adding after a moment's pause, "It is so referred."

assembly?"* In stating the question on an amendment, the chairman should read (1) the passage to be amended; (2) the words to be struck out, if any; (3) the words to be inserted, if any; and (4) the whole passage as it will stand if the amendment is adopted; he then states the question in a form similar to this: "The question is, shall the word *censure* be inserted in the resolution in the place of the word *thanks?*" As soon as a vote is taken, he should immediately state the question then before the assembly, if there be any. Thus, if an amendment has been voted on, the chairman announces the result, and then says: "The question now recurs on the resolution," or, "on the resolution as amended," as the case may be. So, if an amendment is reconsidered, the chairman should announce the result of the vote and state the question before the assembly in a form similar to this: "The motion is carried—the vote on the

---

* In putting the question to vote after stating it, he should add, "As many as are in favor of sustaining the decision of the chair, say *aye*, as many are opposed say *no*." If the ayes have it he should then say, "The ayes have it, and the decision of the chair stands as the judgment of the assembly," or, "the decision of the chair is sustained."

amendment is reconsidered; the question recurs on the adoption of the amendment."*

After stating the question on a motion that can be debated or amended, the chairman, unless some one immediately rises, asks: "Are you ready for the question?"† When the chairman thinks the debate is closed, he again inquires: "Are you ready for the question?" If no one rises, he once more states the question as already described, and puts it to vote.

One of the commonest forms of putting the question (after it has been stated) is this: "As many as are in favor of the motion will say *aye;* those opposed will say *no.*" Another one is as follows: "Those in favor of the motion will hold up the right hand; those opposed will manifest it by the same sign."‡

---

* See § 31 for the method of acting on reports of committees and on a paper containing several paragraphs.

† The question, in some societies, is more usually: "Are there any remarks?" or, "Are there any further remarks?"

‡ See §§ 38, 46-48, 54 for examples of various ways of stating and putting questions, and page 10 for peculiar forms.

PART III.

MISCELLANEOUS.

---

66. The Right of Deliberative Assemblies to Punish their Members.

A deliberative assembly has the inherent right to make and enforce its own laws and punish an offender—the extreme penalty, however, being expulsion from its own body. When expelled, if the assembly is a permanent society, it has a right, for its own protection, to give public notice that the person has ceased to be a member of that society.

But it has no right to go beyond what is necessary for self-protection and publish the charges against the member. In a case where a member of a society was expelled, and an officer of the society published, by their order, a statement of the grave charges upon which he had been found guilty, the expelled member recovered damages from the officer in a suit for libel, the court holding that the truth of the charges did not affect the case.

67. Right of an Assembly to Eject any one from its Place of Meeting.

Every deliberative assembly has the right to decide who may be present during its session; and when the assembly, either by a rule or by a vote, decides that a certain person shall not remain in the room, it is the duty of the chairman to enforce the rule or order, using whatever force is necessary to eject the party.

The chairman can detail members to remove the person, without calling upon the police. If, however, in enforcing the order, any one uses harsher treatment than is necessary to remove the person, the courts have held that he, and he alone, is liable to prosecution, just the same as a policeman would be under similar circumstances. However badly the man may be abused while being removed from the room, neither the chairman nor the society are liable for damages, as, in ordering his removal, they did not exceed their legal rights.

68. Rights of Ecclesiastical Tribunals.

Many of our deliberative assemblies are ecclesiastical bodies, and it is important to know how much respect will be paid to their decisions by the civil courts.

A church became divided, and each party claimed to be the church, and therefore entitled to the church property. The case was taken into the civil courts, and finally, on appeal, to the U. S. Supreme Court, which held the case under advisement for one year, and then reversed the decision of the State Court, because it conflicted with the decision of the highest ecclesiastical court that had acted upon the case. The Supreme Court, in rendering its decision, laid down the broad principle that, when a local church is but a part of a large and more general organization or denomination, the court will accept the decision of the highest ecclesiastical tribunal to which the case has been carried within that general church organization as final, and will not inquire into the justice or injustice of its decree as between the parties before it. The officers, the ministers, the members, or the church body, which the highest judiciary of the denomination recognizes, the court will rec-

ognize. Whom that body expels or cuts
off, the court will hold to be no longer
members of that church.

69. Trial of Members of Societies.

Every deliberative assembly, having the
right to purify its own body, must therefore
have the right to investigate the character
of its members. It can require any of
them to testify in the case, under pain of
expulsion if they refuse.

When the charge is against the member's
character, it is usually referred to a committee of investigation or discipline, or to
some standing committee, to report
upon. Some societies have standing committees, whose duty it is to report cases for
discipline whenever any are known to them.

In either case the committee investigate
the matter and report to the society. This
report need not go into details, but should
contain their recommendations as to what
action the society should take, and should
usually close with resolutions covering the
case, so that there is no need for any one
to offer any additional resolutions upon it.
The ordinary resolutions, where the member is recommended to be expelled, are (1)
to fix the time to which the society shall

adjourn; and (2) to instruct the clerk to cite the member to appear before the society at this adjourned meeting to show cause why he should not be expelled, upon the following charges which should then be given.

After charges are preferred against a member, and the assembly has ordered that he be cited to appear for trial, he is theoretically under arrest, and is deprived of all the rights of membership until his case is disposed of. Without his consent no member should be tried at the same meeting at which the charges are preferred, excepting when the charges relate to something done in that meeting.

The clerk should send the accused a written notice to appear before the society at the time appointed, and should at the same time furnish him with a copy of the charges. A failure to obey the summons is generally cause enough for summary expulsion.

At the appointed meeting what may be called the trial takes place. Frequently the only evidence required against the member is the report of the committee. After it has been read and any additional evidence offered that the committee may see fit to introduce, the accused should be allowed to make an explanation and introduce witnesses, if he so desires. Either party should be allowed to cross-examine the other's witnesses and introduce rebutting testimony. When the evidence is all in, the accused should retire from the room, and the society deliberate upon the question, and finally act by a vote upon the question of expulsion, or other punishment proposed. No member should be expelled by less than a two-thirds* vote—a quorum voting.

In acting upon the case, it must be borne in mind that there is a vast distinction between the evidence necessary to convict in a civil court and that required to convict in an ordinary society or ecclesiastical body. A notorious pickpocket could not even be arrested, much less convicted by a civil court, simply on the ground of being commonly known as a pickpocket; while such evidence would convict and expel him from any ordinary society.

The moral conviction of the truth of the charge is all that is necessary, in an ecclesi-

---

* The U. S. Constitution [Art. 1, Sec. 5] provides that each house of Congress may, "with the concurrence of two-thirds, expel a member."

astical or other deliberative body, to find
the accused guilty of the charges.

If the trial is liable to be long and troublesome, or of a very delicate nature, the member is frequently cited to appear before a
committee, instead of the society, for trial.
In this case the committee report to the society the result of their trial of the case,
with resolutions covering the punishment
which they recommend the society to adopt.
When the committee's report is read, the
accused should be permitted to make his
statement of the case, the committee being
allowed to reply. The accused then retires
from the room, and the society acts upon the
resolutions submitted by the committee. The
members of the committee should vote upon
the case the same as other members.

If the accused wishes counsel at his trial,
it is usual to allow it, provided the counsel
is a member of the society in good standing. Should the counsel be guilty of improper conduct during the trial, the society
can refuse to hear him, and can also punish
him.

70. Call of the House.

The object of a call of the house is to
compel the attendance of absent members,

and is allowable only in assemblies that have the power to compel the attendance of absentees. It is usual to provide that when no quorum is present, a small number [one-fifth of the members elect in Congress*] can order a call of the house. To prevent this privilege from being used improperly, it is well to provide that when the call is made the members cannot adjourn or dispense with further proceedings in the call until a quorum is obtained. A rule like the following would answer for city councils and other similar bodies that have the power to enforce attendance:

Rule. When no quorum is present, members may order a call of the house and compel the attendance of absent members. After the call is

---

* In the early history of our Congress a call of the house required a day's notice, and in the English Parliament it is usual to order that the call shall be made on a certain day in the future, usually not over ten days afterwards, though it has been as long as six weeks afterwards. The object of this is to give notice so that all the members may be present on that day, when important business is to come before the house. In Congress a call of the house is only used now when no quorum is present, and as soon as a quorum appears it is usual to dispense with further proceedings in the call, and this is in order at any stage of the proceedings. In some of our legislative bodies proceedings in the call cannot be dispensed with except a majority of the members elect vote in favor of so doing. In Congress it is customary afterwards to remit the fees that have been assessed.

ordered, a motion to adjourn, or to dispense with
further proceedings in the call, cannot be entertained until a quorum is present, or until the
sergeant-at-arms reports that in his opinion no
quorum can be obtained on that day.

If no quorum is present a call of the
house takes precedence of everything, even
reading the minutes, except the motion to
adjourn, and only requires in its favor the
number specified in the rule. If a quorum is
present a call should rank with questions of
privilege [§ 12], requiring a majority vote
for its adoption, and if rejected it should
not be renewed, while a quorum is present, at that meeting [see first note to § 42].
After a call is ordered, until further proceedings in the call are dispensed with, no
motion is in order except to adjourn and a
motion relating to the call, so that a recess
could not be taken by unanimous consent.
An adjournment puts an end to all proceedings in the call, except that the assembly before adjournment, if a quorum is
present, can order such members as are already arrested to make their excuses at an
adjourned meeting.

Proceedings in a Call of the House. When
the call is ordered the clerk calls the roll of
members alphabetically, noting the absentees; he then calls over again the names

of absentees, when excuses* can be made; after this the doors are locked, no one being permitted to leave, and an order similar in form to the following is adopted: "That the Sergeant-at-Arms take into custody, and bring to the bar of the House, such of its members as are absent without the leave of the House." A warrant signed by the presiding officer and attested by the clerk, with a list of absentees attached, is then given to the sergeant-at-arms,† who immediately proceeds to arrest the absentees. When he appears with members under arrest, he proceeds to the chairman's desk (being announced by the doorkeeper in large bodies), followed by the arrested members, and makes his return. The chairman arraigns each member separately, and asks

---

* It is usual in Congress to excuse those who have "paired off," that is, two members on opposite sides of the pending question who have agreed that both will stay away. In order to "pair off," the absence of both parties must not affect the result, which would rarely be the case in municipal bodies like those under consideration.

† "It shall be the duty of the Sergeant-at-Arms to attend the House during its sittings; to aid in the enforcement of order, under the direction of the Speaker; to execute the commands of the House from time to time; together with all such process, issued by authority thereof, as shall be directed to him by the Speaker." (Rule 22 H. R.) The words "Sergeant-at-Arms" can be replaced in the order by "Chief of Police," or whatever officer is to serve the process.

what excuse he has to offer for being absent from the sittings of the assembly without its leave.   The member states his excuse, and a motion is made that he be discharged from custody and admitted to
his seat either without payment of fees or
after paying the fees. Until a member has
paid the fees assessed against him he cannot vote or be recognized by the chair for
any purpose.

INDEX.

The figures refer usually to where the treatment of the subject begins. Always consult the Table of Rules, p. 8, for information about any particular motion. A complete list of motions will be found in the Index, under the title, " Motions, list of." The arrangement of the work can be most easily seen by examining the Table of Contents [pp. 3-6]; its plan is explained in the Introduction, pp. 20-23.

PAGE

Adjourn, motion to, ... 37, 191
    effect upon unfinished business, ... 37
    in committee [see, *Rise, motion to*] . . 37, 83, 94, 95
    motion to " fix the time to which to adjourn, . 36, 191

Adopt, Accept or Agree, ... 88

Amendment, motion to " amend," . . . 65, 176
    by " adding," or " inserting," . . . 66, 67
    by " striking out," 66, 176
    by " striking out and inserting," . . . 66
    by " substituting," 67
    by " dividing the question," . . 30, 31, 67
    of an amendment, ... 66
    in committee, ... 81, 170
    of reports or propositions with several paragraphs, 91, 153
    of Rules of Order, By-Laws and Constitutions, . 138
    motions that cannot be amended, . 8, 69, 177
    examples of improper amendments, . . 69

Announcing the Vote, . . . 110, 113, 173

Appeal from the decision of the chair, . . 45, 189

Apply, meaning of, ... 22

Assembly, how organized, . . . 139-155
    the word to be replaced by Society, Convention,
       etc., when it occurs in forms of questions, . 24
    right to punish members, ... 198
    right to eject persons from their room, . . 199
    trial of members, ... 201

Ayes and Noes [same as *Yeas and Nays*], . . 114

Ballot, ... 113

                                                                    PAGE
Blanks, filling of, ...   68
   in balloting, not to be counted, ...   114

Boards, of Trustees, Managers, etc., reports of, in order
        when reports of standing committees are made,   137
   [See *Quorum*.]

Business, introduction of, ... 25–32, 172
   order of, ...   137
   priority of, questions relating to are undebatable,   101
   unfinished, effect of an adjournment upon, . .   37

By-Laws, what they should contain, . . .   155
   adoption of, ...   153
   amendment of, ...   138
   suspension of [Note]   50

Call of the House, ...   204

Call to Order, ...   46, 188

Chairman, duties of, ... 119, 159
   election of, ...   139
   temporary, ...   122, 147
   right to vote when it affects result, . . .   112, 121
   of a committee, ...   80, 170
   of committee of the whole, ...   94
   inexperienced, hints to, ...   160

Change of Vote allowed before result is announced, .   111

Classification of Motions according to their object,   174
   into Privileged, Incidental, Subsidiary and Prin-
     cipal, ...   32 35

Clerk [see *Secretary*].

Close Debate, motion to, ...   106, 179, 181

Commit, motion to, ...   63, 177

Committees, appointment of, ...   64, 143
   how they should be composed, . . .   65, 169
   chairman of, ...   80, 144, 162
   object of, ...   79, 169, 177
   quorum in, consists of a majority, . .   81, 136
   quorum in Committee of the Whole, same as in
     Assembly, ...   136
   manner of conducting business in, . .   81, 170

Committees, *continued.*   PAGE
                                                         84, 171
  Reports of, their form,   85, 144
    their reception,   88, 145
    their adoption,   137
    their place in the order of business,   86
    common errors in acting upon [Note]
  Minority Reports of, their form,   84, 171
    cannot be acted upon unless moved as a substi-
    tute for the committee's (majority's) report, 82, 171
    select and standing, distinction between,   80
  of the whole,   93
  as if in committee of the whole,   96

Congress, rules of, the basis of this work,   18–20

Consent, unanimous [same as *General*],   50, 51, 114
  can be given only when a quorum is present [Note], 135

Consideration of a question, objection to,   47, 182

Constitutions, what they should contain,   155
  adoption of, by a society,   153
  amendment of,   138
  cannot be suspended [Note]   50

Convention, organizing and conducting a meeting of,   146

Credentials of delegates,   147

Debate, what precedes,   29, 172
  no member to speak but twice in same.   99, 193
  no speech to be longer than ten minutes.   100, 193
  number and length of speeches in Congress [Note] 100, 193
  member reporting measure has right to close,   100
  list of *undebatable* questions,   101
  motions that open the main question to,   102
  principles regulating the extent of [Note]   103
  decorum in,   104, 193
  closing, or limiting.   106, 179–182
  limits of, can be extended by a ⅔ vote,   100, 117

Decorum in debate,   104, 193

Definitions of various terms.   22, 23

Delegates, organization of a meeting of,   146

Dilatory motions not permitted,   124

	PAGE
Disorderly words in debate, ...	105
Division of the assembly, . . .	110
of questions [see *Amendment*, . - . 30. 67, 176
Duties of Officers [see *Chairman, Secretary* and *Treasurer*]	
Ecclesiastical Tribunals, legal rights of, . .	199
Eject persons from their room, right of an assembly to,	199
Election of Officers, ... 139, 146, 147	
Errors, common, . . 23 and notes on pp. 86, 123, 124	
in amendments [Note]	69
Ex-officio [Note]	79
Explanation, personal, unprivileged [Note], .	190
Expulsion of Members requires a ⅔ vote, . .	203
Expunge [Note]	71
Extend the limits of debate, ... 100, 117	
Filling blanks, ...	68
Fix the time to which to Adjourn, motion to. . 36, 191	
Floor, how to obtain, ... 25, 172	
necessary to obtain in order to make a motion [Note], 28	
Forms of making motions, ...	172
of a resolution, ...	172
of stating and putting questions, . . 10, 109, 194	
of announcing the result of a vote, . 110, 113, 173	
of acting on reports of committees, . . 85, 88, 144	
of acting on reports or resolutions containing several paragraphs, ... 90, 153	
of reports of committees, ... 84, 171	
of treasurers' reports, ...	168
of minutes of a meeting, ... 126, 164	
of conducting an occasional or mass meeting, .	139
of conducting a meeting of delegates, . .	146
of conducting a meeting to organize a society, .	149
of conducting an ordinary meeting of a society, .	152
General Consent [see *Consent, unanimous*].	
Hints to Inexperienced Chairmen, . . .	160

PAGE

House, call of the, ... 204

Incidental questions, ... 34

Indecorum, leave to continue speaking after, . 47, 105

Indefinite postponement, ... 70, 183

Informal consideration of a question, . . . 96

Introduction of Business, . . . 25-32, 172

Journal [see *Minutes*].

Lay on the table, motion to. . . . 51, 178, 183

Legal Rights [see *Assembly* and *Ecclesiastical Tribunals*].

Limit debate, motion to, ... 108, 117

Main question, ... 32

Majority [see *Two-thirds* and *Quorum*].

Meeting, distinction between it and *session* [Note] . 131
    how to conduct [see *Forms*].

Members not to be present during a debate concerning
    themselves, ... 106
    not to vote on questions personal to themselves, . 112
    trial of, ... 201
    not to be expelled by less than a two-thirds vote, . 203

Minority Report [see *Committees*].

Minutes, form and contents of, . . . 126, 162, 164
    correction of, ... 127

Moderator [see *Chairman*].

Modification of a motion by the mover, . 30, 32, 49

Motions, list of. [For details see each motion in the index].
    adjourn, ... 37, 191
    adjourn, fix the time to which to, . . 36, 191
    adopt a report [same as *accept* or *agree to*], . 88, 145
    amend, ... 65, 176
    appeal, ... 45, 189
    blanks, filling, ... 68
    call to order, ... 46, 188
    close debate, ... 106, 179-182
    commit, ... 63, 177
    consideration of a question, objection to, . 47, 182

Motions, list of, *continued.*

	PAGE
divide the question,	30, 67, 176
expunge [Note]	71
extend the limits of debate,	100, 117, 193
fix the time to which to adjourn,	36, 191
incidental motions or questions,	34
indefinitely postpone,	70, 183
informal consideration of a question,	96
lay on the table,	51, 178, 183
leave to continue speech when guilty of indecorum,	105, 189
leave to withdraw a motion,	49
limit debate,	106, 181
main motions or questions,	32
objection to the consideration of a question,	47, 182
order, questions of,	46, 188
orders of the day,	41, 186
orders, special,	42, 187
postpone to a certain day,	62, 178
postpone indefinitely,	70, 183
previous question,	55, 179
principal motions or questions,	32
priority of business, questions relating to,	101
privileged motions or questions,	35
privilege, questions of,	40, 190
reading papers,	48
reception of a report [see *Committees*].	85, 144
recommit [same as Commit],	63, 177
reconsider,	73, 184
refer [same as Commit],	63, 177
renewal of a motion,	70, 186
rescind,	71
rise [in committee, equals adjourn],	37, 83, 94, 95
shall the question be considered [or discussed] ?	47, 182
special order, to make a,	42, 187
strike out [see *Amendment*],	66, 176
subsidiary motions or questions,	33
substitute [one form of *Amendment*, which see]	67, 176
suspension of the Rules,	50, 188
take from the table [see *Lay on the Table*],	52, 179

Motions, list of, *continued.*

PAGE

take up a question out of its proper order, . 137

withdrawal of a motion, ... 49

Motions, Table of Rules relating to, . . . 8

classified according to their object, . . 175

classified into Privileged, Incidental, Subsidiary, etc., 32–35

order of precedence of [see each motion, §§ 10–27], . 10

how to be made, . . . 25–29, 139–143, 172

a second required [with certain exceptions], . 29, 194

to be stated by chairman before being discussed, 29, 173

when to be in writing, ... 30, 172

how to be divided, ... 30, 67

how to be modified by the mover, . . 30, 32, 49

how to be stated and put to the question, . 109, 194

that are in order when another has the floor, . 28

that do not have to be seconded, . . 30

that *cannot be amended,* . . . 8, 69, 177

that *cannot be debated,* 101

that open main question to debate, . . 102

that require two-thirds vote for their adoption, . 116

dilatory, not allowed, ... 124

Nominations, how treated, . . . 68, 140, 141

closing, effect of, ... 113

Numbers of paragraphs, clerk to correct without a vote, 68

Objection to the consideration [discussion or introduction] of a question, ... 47, 182

Obtaining the floor, ... 25

Officers of an assembly [See *Chairman, Secretary, Treasurer* and *Vice-President*].

election of, ... 139

temporary, ... 146, 147

Order, questions of and a call to, . . . 46, 188

of business, ... 137

of the day, ... 41, 186

special, ... 42, 187

of precedence of motions [see *Precedence*]

	PAGE
Organization of an occasional or mass meeting,	139
of a convention or assembly of delegates,	146
of a permanent society,	149
Papers and documents, reading of,	48
in custody of Secretary,	130, 165
Parliamentary Law, its origin, etc.,	17
Personal explanation, not privileged [Note]	190
Plan of the Manual,	20–23
Postpone to a certain time,	62, 178
indefinitely,	70, 183
Preamble, considered after the rest of a paper,	92
Precedence of motions [see each motion, §§ 10–27],	10
meaning of,	22
Presiding Officer [see *Chairman*].	
Previous question,	55, 179
Principal (or main) question,	32
Priority of Business, questions relating to, are unde-batable,	101
Privilege, questions of,	40, 190
Privileged questions,	35
Programme of a meeting [same as *orders of the day*]	42
Putting the question, form of,	109, 197
Questions [see *Forms, Motions, Privilege, Privileged, Order, Stating* and *Putting*].	
Quorum, when there is no rule, consists of a majority,	135
committees and boards cannot decide upon,	136
in Congress and Parliament [Note].	135
Reading of Papers,	48
Reception of a report [see *Committees*].	85
Recess,	39
Recommit [same as Commit],	63, 177
Reconsider,	73, 184
Record, or minutes.	125, 162
Recording officer [see *Secretary*].	

PAGE

Refer [same as Commit], ... 63, 177

Renewal of a motion, ... 70, 186

Reports of committees [see *Committees*].

Rescind, ... 71, 132

Resolutions, forms of, ... 172
    not in order if they conflict with Constitution, By-
      Laws or Rules of Order, . . . 159

Rights of assemblies [see *Assembly*].
    of ecclesiastical tribunals, ... 200

Rise, motion to, in committee, equals adjourn, 37, 83, 94, 95

Rules of Debate [see *Debate*], . . . 98–108, 193
    of Order, amendment of, ... 138
    of Order, what they should contain, . . 158, 159
    standing, what they should contain, . . 158
    suspension of, ... 50, 188
    relating to motions, Table of, . . . 8–10

Seconding, motions that do not require, . . 30, 194

Secretary, duties of, ... 125, 162
    additional duties of, when receiving money, 165
    election of, ... 140

Session, ... 131

Shall the question be considered [or discussed]? . 47, 182

Speaking, Rules of [see *Debate*], . . 98, 104, 193

Special Order, ... 42, 187

Standing Rules, ... 158

Stating a Question, form of, . . . 109, 194

Strike Out [see *Amendment*] . . . 66, 176

Subsidiary motions or questions, . . . 33

Substitute [see *Amendment*] . . . 67, 176

Sum, smallest, first put, ... 68

Suspension of the Constitution or By-Laws [Note], . 50
    of the Rules, ... 50, 188
    of the Standing Rules, ... 50, 158

Table of Rules, relating to motions. . . 8–10

PAGE

Table, motion to lay on the, . . . 51, 178, 183
    motion to take from the, ... 52
Tellers, ... 110, 113
Time, longest, first put, ... 68
Treasurer, duties of, ... 165
Trial of Members, ... 201
Two-thirds vote, motions requiring, . . . 116
    various kinds of, explained [Note], . . 116
    principles regulating [Note], ... 117
Unanimous Consent, [see *Consent, Unanimous*].
Undebatable Questions, ... 101
Unfinished Business, effect of adjournment upon, . 37
    its place in the order of business, . . . 137
Vice-Presidents, ... 146
Vote, various methods of putting the question, . 109, 194
    various methods of voting, . . . 109–116
    forms of announcing, . . 109, 113, 115, 173
    change of, permitted before result is announced, . 111
    effect of a tie, ... 112
    motions requiring more than a majority, . 116
    plurality, ... 110, 116
    chairman entitled to when it affects result, . 112, 121
Whole, Committee of the, ... 93
Withdrawal of a Motion, ... 49
Yeas and Nays, voting by, ... 114
Yields, meaning of, ... 22